DOVER·THRIFT·EDITIONS

Native American Myths

LEWIS SPENCE

DOVER PUBLICATIONS, INC.
Mineola, New York

DOVER THRIFT EDITIONS

GENERAL EDITOR: MARY CAROLYN WALDREP
EDITOR OF THIS VOLUME: DAVID DUTKANICZ

Bibliographical Note

This Dover edition, first published in 2005, is an excerpt from *Myths and Legends of the North American Indians* originally published by Thomas Y. Crowell Company, New York, in 1914. The excerpt comprises the text of chapters III–VII, and includes the map (now on page iv) that was originally on page 361.

Library of Congress Cataloging-in-Publication Data

Spence, Lewis, 1874–1955.
 [Myths of the North American Indians. Chapter 3–7]
 Native American myths / Lewis Spence.
  p. cm.
 "An excerpt of chapters III–VII of Myths and legends of the North American Indians [i.e. The myths of the North American Indians] originally published by Thomas Y. Crowell Company, New York, in 1914"—T.p. verso.
 ISBN 0-486-44573-9 (pbk.)
  1. Indian mythology—North America. 2. Indians of North America—Folklore.
I. Title.

E98.R3S7 2005
299.7'113—dc22

2005052625

Manufactured in the United States of America
Dover Publications, Inc., 31 East 2nd Street, Mineola, N.Y. 11501

Contents

CHAPTER   PAGE

Map to Illustrate the Linguistic Families of
North American Indians   iv

I   Algonquian Myths and Legends   1

II   Iroquois Myths and Legends   50

III Sioux Myths and Legends   81

IV   Myths and Legends of the Pawnees   106

V   Myths and Legends of the Northern and
Northwestern Indians   111

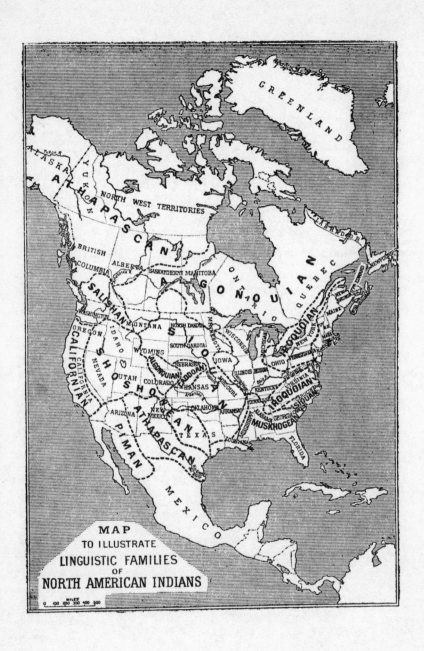

MAP
TO ILLUSTRATE
LINGUISTIC FAMILIES
OF
NORTH AMERICAN INDIANS

I

ALGONQUIAN MYTHS AND LEGENDS

GLOOSKAP AND MALSUM

THE ALGONQUIN Indians have perhaps a more extensive mythology than the majority of Indian peoples, and as they have been known to civilization or several centuries their myths have the advantage of having been thoroughly examined.

One of the most interesting figures in their pantheon is Glooskap, which means "The Liar"; but so far from an affront being intended to deity by this appellation, it was bestowed as a compliment to his craftiness, cunning being regarded as one of the virtues by all savage peoples.

Glooskap and is brother Malsum, the Wolf, were twins, and from this we may infer that they were the opposites of a dualistic system, Glooskap standing for what seems "good" to the savage, and Malsum for all that was "bad."[1] Their mother died at their birth, and out of her body Glooskap formed the sun and moon, animals, fishes, and the human race, while the malicious Malsum made mountains, valleys, serpents, and every manner of thing which he considered would inconvenience the race of men.

Each of the brothers possessed a secret as to what would kill him, as do many other beings in myth and fairy story, notably Llew Llaw Gyffes in Welsh romance.

Malsum asked Glooskap in what manner he could be killed, and the elder brother, to try his sincerity, replied that the only way in which his life could be taken was by the touch of an owl's feather—or, as some variants of the myth say, by that of a flowering rush. Malsum in his turn confided to Glooskap that he could only perish by a blow from a fern-root. The malicious Wolf, taking his bow, brought down an owl, and while Glooskap slept struck him with a feather plucked from its wing. Glooskap immediately expired, but to Malsum's chagrin came to life

---

[1] This "goodness" and "badness," however, is purely relative and of modern origin, such deities, as already explained, being figures in a light-and-darkness myth.

again. This tale is surprisingly reminiscent of the Scandinavian myth of Balder, who would only die if struck by a sprig of mistletoe by his brother Hodur. Like Baldur, Glooskap is a sun-god, as is well proved by the circumstance that when he dies he does not fail to revive.

But Malsum resolved to learn his brother's secret and to destroy him at the first opportunity. Glooskap had told him subsequently to his first attempt that only a pine-root could kill him, and with this Malsum struck him while he slept as before, but Glooskap, rising up and laughing, drove Malsum into the forest, and seated himself by a stream, where he murmured, as if musing to himself: "Only a flowering rush can kill me." Now he said this because he knew that Quah-beet, the Great Beaver, was hidden among the rushes on the bank of the stream and would hear every word he uttered. The Beaver went at once to Malsum and told him what he regarded as is brother's vital secret. The wicked Malsum was so glad that he promised to give the Beaver whatever he might ask for. But when the beast asked for wings like a pigeon Malsum burst into mocking laughter and cried: "Ho, you with the tail like a file, what need have you of wings?" At this the Beaver was wroth, and, going to Glooskap, made a clean breast of what he had done. Glooskap, now thoroughly infuriated, dug up a fern-root, and, rushing into the recesses of the forest, sought out his treacherous brother and with a blow of the fatal plant struck him dead.

SCANDINAVIAN ANALOGIES

But although Malsum was slain he subsequently appears in the Algonquian myth as Lox, or Loki, the chief of the wolves, a mischievous and restless spirit. In his account of the Algonquian mythology Charles Godfrey Leland appears to think that the entire system has been sophisticated by Norse mythology filtering through the Eskimo. Although the probabilities are against such a theory, there are many points in common between the two systems, as we shall see later, and among them few are more striking than the fact that the Scandinavian and Algonquian evil influences possess one and the same name.

When Glooskap had completed the world he made man and the smaller supernatural beings, such as fairies and dwarfs. He formed man from the trunk of an ash-tree, and the elves from its bark. Like Odin, he trained two birds to bring him the news of the world, but their absences were so prolonged that he selected a black and a white wolf as his attendants. He waged a strenuous and exterminating warfare on the evil monsters which then infested the world, and on the sorcerers and witches who were harmful to man. He levelled the hills and restrained the forces of nature in his mighty struggles, in which he towered to giant stature, his head and shoulders rising high above the clouds. Yet in his dealings with men he was gentle and quietly humorous, not to say ingenuous.

On one occasion he sought out a giant sorcerer named Win-pe, one of the most powerful of the evil influences then dwelling upon the earth. Win-pe shot upward till his head was above the tallest pine of the forest, but Glooskap, with a god-like laugh, grew till his head reached the stars, and tapped the wizard gently with the butt of his bow, so that he fell dead at his feet.

But although he exterminated many monsters and placed a check upon the advance of the forces of evil, Glooskap did not find that the race of men grew any better or wiser. In fact, the more he accomplished on their behalf the worse they became, until at last they reached such a pitch of evil conduct that the god resolved to quit the world altogether. But, with a feeling of consideration still for the beings he had created, he announced that within the next seven years he would grant to all and sundry any request they might make. A great many people were desirous of profiting by this offer, but it was with the utmost difficulty that they could discover where Glooskap was. Those who did find him and who chose injudiciously were severely punished, while those whose desires were reasonable were substantially rewarded.

GLOOSKAP'S GIFTS

Four Indians who went to Glooskap's abode found it a place of magical delights, a land fairer than the mind could conceive. Asked by the god what had brought them thither, one replied that his heart was evil and that anger had made him its slave, but that he wished to be meek and pious. The second, a poor man, desired to be rich, and the third, who was of low estate and despised by the folk of his tribe, wished to be universally honoured and respected. The fourth was a vain man, conscious of his good looks, whose appearance was eloquent of conceit. Although he was tall, he had stuffed fur into his moccasins to make him appear still taller, and his wish was that he might become bigger than any man of his tribe and that he might live for ages.

Glooskap drew four small boxes from his medicine-bag and gave one to each, desiring that they should not open them until they reached home. When the first three arrived at their respective lodges each opened his box, and found therein an unguent of great fragrance and richness, with which he rubbed himself. The wicked man became meek and patient, the poor man speedily grew wealthy, and the despised man became stately and respected. But the conceited man had stopped on his way home in a clearing in the woods, and, taking out his box, had anointed himself with the ointment it contained. His wish also was granted, but not exactly in the manner he expected, for he was changed into a pine-tree, the first of the species, and the tallest tree of the forest at that.

GLOOSKAP AND THE BABY

Glooskap, having conquered the Kewawkqu', a race of giants and magicians, and the Medecolin, who were cunning sorcerers, and Pamola, a wicked spirit of the night, besides hosts of fiends, goblins, cannibals, and witches, felt himself great indeed, and boasted to a certain woman that there was nothing left for him to subdue.

But the woman laughed and said: "Are you quite sure, Master? There is still one who remains unconquered, and nothing can overcome him."

In some surprise Glooskap inquired the name of this mighty individual.

"He is called Wasis," replied the woman; "but I strongly advise you to have no dealings with him."

Wasis was only a baby, who sat on the floor sucking a piece of maple-sugar and crooning a little song to himself. Now Glooskap had never married and was quite ignorant of how children are managed, but with perfect confiedence he smiled to the baby and asked it to come to him. The baby smiled back to him, but never moved, whereupon Glooskap imitated the beautiful song of a certain bird. Wasis, however, paid no heed to him, but went on sucking his maple-sugar. Glooskap, unaccustomed to such treatment, lashed himself into a furious rage, and in terrible and threatening accents ordered Wasis to come crawling to him at once. But Wasis burst into direful howling, which quite drowned the god's thunderous accents, and for all the threatenings of the deity he would not budge. Glooskap, now thoroughly aroused, brought all his magical resources to his aid. He recited the most terrible spells, the most dreadful incantations. He sang the songs which raise the dead, and which sent the devil scurrying to the nethermost depths of the pit. But Wasis evidently seemed to think this was all some sort of a game, for he merely smiled wearily and looked a trifle bored. At last Glooskap in despair rushed from the hut, while Wasis, sitting on the floor, cried, "Goo, goo," and crowed triumphantly. And to this day the Indians say that when a baby cries "Goo" he remembers the time when he conquered the mighty Glooskap.

GLOOSKAP'S FAREWELL

At length the day on which Glooskap was to leave the earth arrived, and to celebrate the event he caused a great feast to be made on the shores of Lake Minas. It was attended by all the animals, and when it drew to a close Glooskap entered his great canoe and slowly drifted out of sight. When they could see him no longer they still heard his beautiful singing growing fainter and fainter in the distance, until at last it died away altogether. Then a strange thing happened. The beasts, who up to this time had spoken but one language, could no longer understand each other, and in confusion fled away, never again to meet in friendly converse until Glooskap shall return and revive the halcyon days of the Golden Age.

This tradition of Glooskap strikingly recalls that of the Mexican god Quetzalcoatl, who drifted from the shores of Mexico eastward toward the fabled land of Tlapallan, whence he had originally come. Glooskap, like the Mexican deity alluded to, is, as has already been indicated, a sun-god, or, more properly speaking, a son of the sun, who has come to earth on a mission of enlightenment and civilization, to render the world habitable for mankind and to sow the seeds of the arts, domestic and agricultural. Quetzalcoatl disappeared toward the east because it was the original home of his father, the sun, and not toward the west, which is merely the sun's resting-place for the night. But Glooskap drifted westward, as most sun-children do.

HOW GLOOSKAP CAUGHT THE SUMMER

A very beautiful myth tells how Glooskap captured the Summer. The form in which it is preserved is a kind of poetry possessing something in the nature of metre, which until a few generations ago was recited by many Algonquian firesides. A long time ago Glooskap wandered very far north to the Ice-country, and, feeling tired and cold, sought shelter at a wigwam where dwelt a great giant—the giant Winter. Winter received the god hospitably, filled a pipe of tobacco for him, and entertained him with charming stories of the old time as he smoked. All the time Winter was casting his spell over Glooskap, for as he talked drowsily and monotonously he gave forth a freezing atmosphere, so that Glooskap first dozed and then fell into a deep sleep—the heavy slumber of the winter season. For six whole months he slept; then the spell of the frost arose from his brain and he awoke. He took his way homeward and southward, and the farther south he fared the warmer it felt, and the flowers began to spring up around his steps.

At length he came to a vast, trackless forest, where, under primeval trees, many little people were dancing. The queen of these folk was Summer, a most exquisitely beautiful, if very tiny, creature. Glooskap caught the queen up in his great hand, and, cutting a long lasso from the hide of a moose, secured it round her tiny frame. Then he ran away, letting the cord trail loosely behind him.

THE ELVES OF LIGHT

The tiny people, who were the Elves of Light, came clamouring shrilly after him, pulling frantically at the lasso. But as Glooskap ran the cord ran out, and pull as they might they were left far behind.

Northward he journeyed once more, and came to the wigwam of

Winter. The giant again received him hospitably, and began to tell the old stories whose vague charm had exercised such a fascination upon the god. But Glooskap in his turn began to speak. Summer was lying in his bosom, and her strength and heat sent forth such powerful magic that at length Winter began to show signs of distress. The sweat poured profusely down his face, and gradually he commenced to melt, as did his dwelling. Then slowly nature awoke, the song of birds was heard, first faintly, then more clearly and joyously. The thin green shoots of the young grass appeared, and the dead leaves of last autumn were carried down to the river by the melting snow. Lastly the fairies came out, and Glooskap, leaving Summer with them, once more bent his steps southward.

This is obviously a nature-myth conceived by a people dwelling in a climate where the rigours of winter gave way for a more or less brief space only to the blandishments of summer. To them winter was a giant, and summer an elf of pigmy proportions. The stories told during the winter season are eloquent of the life led by people dwelling in a sub-arctic climate, where the traditional tale, the father of epic poetry, whiles away the long dark hours, while the winter tempest roars furiously without and the heaped-up snow renders the daily occupation of the hunter impossible.

GLOOSKAP'S WIGWAM

The Indians say that Glooskap lives far away, no one knows where, in a very great wigwam. His chief occupation is making arrows, and it would appear that each of these stands for a day. One side of his wigwam is covered with arrows, and when his lodge shall be filled with them the last great day will arrive. Then he will call upon his army of good spirits and go forth to attack Malsum in a wonderful canoe, which by magical means can be made to expand so as to hold an army or contract so that it may be carried in the palm of the hand. The war with his evil brother will be one of extermination, and not one single individual on either side will be left. But the good will go to Glooskap's beautiful abode, and all will be well at last.

THE SNOW-LODGE

Chill breezes had long forewarned the geese of the coming cold season, and the constant cry from above of "Honk, honk," told the Indians that the birds' migration was in progress.

The buffalo-hunters of the Blackfeet, an Algonquian tribe, were abroad with the object of procuring the thick robes and the rich meat which would keep them warm and provide good fare through the desolate winter moons. Sacred Otter had been lucky. Many buffaloes had fallen to him, and he was busily occupied in skinning them. But while the braves plied the knife quickly and deftly they heeded not the dun, lowering clouds heavy with tempest hanging like a black curtain over the northern horizon. Suddenly the clouds swooped down from their place in the heavens like a flight of black eagles, and with a roar the blizzard was upon them.

Sacred Otter and his son crouched beneath the carcass of a dead buffalo for shelter. But the air was frore as water in which the ice is floating, and he knew that they would quickly perish unless they could find some better protection from the bitter wind. So he made a small *tepee,* or tent, out of the buffalo's hide, and both crawled inside. Against this crazy shelter the snow quickly gathered and drifted, so that soon the inmates of the tiny lodge sank into a comfortable drowse induced by the gentle warmth. As Sacred Otter slept he dreamed. Away in the distance he described a great *tepee,* crowned with a colour like the gold of sunlight, and painted with a cluster of stars symbolic of the North. The ruddy disc of the sun was pictured at the back, and to this was affixed the tail of the Sacred Buffalo. The skirts of the *tepee* were painted to represent ice, and on its side had been drawn four yellow legs with a green claws, typical of the Thunder-bird. A buffalo in glaring red frowned above the door, and bunches of crow-feathers, with small bells attached, swung and tinkled in the breeze.

Sacred Otter, surprised at the unusual nature of the paintings, stood before the *tepee* lost in admiration of its decorations, when he was startled to hear a voice say:

"Who walks round my *tepee?* Come in—come in!"

THE LORD OF COLD WEATHER

Sacred Otter entered, and beheld a tall, white-haired man, clothed all in white, sitting at the back of the lodge, of which he was the sole occupant. Sacred Otter took a seat, but the owner of the *tepee* never looked his way, smoking on in stolid silence. Before him was an earthen altar, on which was laid juniper, as in the Sun ceremonial. His face was painted yellow, with a red line in the region of the mouth, and another across the eyes to the ears. Across his breast he wore a mink-skin, and round his waist small strips of otterskin, to all of which bells were attached. For a long time he kept silence, but at length he laid down his black stone pipe and addressed Sacred Otter as follows:

"I am Es-tonea-pesta, the Lord of Cold Weather, and this, my dwelling, is the Snow-tepee, or Yellow Paint Lodge. I control and send the driving snow and biting winds from the Northland. You are here because I have taken pity upon you, and on your son who was caught in the blizzard with you. Take this Snow-tepee with its symbols and medicines. Take also this mink-skin tobacco-pouch, this black stone pipe, and my supernatural power. You must make a *tepee* similar to this on your return to camp."

The Lord of Cold Weather then minutely explained to Sacred Otter the symbols of which he must make use in painting the lodge, and gave him the songs and ceremonial connected with it. At this juncture Sacred Otter awoke. He observed that the storm had abated somewhat, and as soon as it grew fair enough he and his son crawled from their shelter and tramped home waist-high through the soft snow. Sacred Otter spent the long, cold nights in making a model of the Snow-tepee and painting it as he had been directed in his dream. He also collected the "medicines" necessary for the ceremonial, and in the spring, when new lodges were made, he built and painted the Snow-tepee.

The power of Sacred Otter waxed great because of his possession of the Snow-lodge which the Lord of Cold had vouchsafed to him in dream. Soon was it proved. Once more while hunting buffalo he and several companions were caught in a blizzard when many a weary mile from camp. They appealed to Sacred Otter to utilize the "medicine" of the Lord of Cold. Directing that several women and children who were with the party should be placed on sledges, and that the men should go in advance and break a passage through the snow for the horses, he took the mink tobacco-pouch and the black stone pipe he had received from the Cold-maker and commenced to smoke. He blew the smoke in the direction whence the storm came and prayed to the Lord of Cold to have pity on the people. Gradually the storm-clouds broke and cleared and on every side the blue sky was seen. The people hastened on, as they knew the blizzard was only being held back for a space. But their camp was at hand, and they soon reached it in safety.

Never again, however, would Sacred Otter use his mystic power. For he dreaded that he might offend the Lord of Cold. And who could afford to do that?

THE STAR-MAIDEN

A pretty legend of the Chippeways, an Algonquian tribe, tells how Algon, a hunter, won for his bride the daughter of a star. While walking over the prairies he discovered a circular pathway, worn as if by the tread of many feet, though there were no foot-marks visible outside its bounds. The young hunter, who had never before encountered one of these "fairy rings," was filled with surprise at the discovery, and hid himself in the long grass to see whether an explanation might not be forthcoming. He had not long to wait. In a little while he heard the sound of music, so faint and sweet that it surpassed anything he had ever dreamed of. The strains grew fuller and richer, and as they seemed to come from above he turned his eyes toward the sky. Far in the blue he could see a tiny white speck like a floating cloud. Nearer and nearer it came, and the astonished hunter saw that it was no cloud, but a dainty osier car, in which were seated twelve beautiful maidens. The music he had heard was the sound of their voices as they sang strange and magical songs. Descending into the charmed ring, they danced round and round with such exquisite grace and abandon that it was a sheer delight to watch them. But after the first moments of dazzled surprise Algon had eyes only for the youngest of the group, a slight, vivacious creature, so fragile and delicate that it seemed to the stalwart hunter that a breath would blow her away.

He was, indeed, seized with a fierce passion for the dainty sprite, and he speedily decided to spring from the grass and carry her off. But the pretty creatures were too quick for him. The fairy of his choice of skillfully eluded his grasp and rushed to the car. The others followed, and in a moment they were soaring up in the air, singing a sweet, unearthly song. The disconsolate hunter returned to his lodge, but try as he might he could not get the thought of the Star-maiden out of his head, and next day, long before the hours of the fairies' arrival, he lay in the grass awaiting the sweet sounds that would herald their approach. At length the car appeared. The twelve ethereal beings danced as before. Again Algon made a desperate attempt to seize the youngest, and again he was unsuccessful.

"Let us stay," said one of the Star-maidens. "Perhaps the mortal wishes to teach us his earthly dances." But the youngest sister would not hear of it, and they all rose out of sight in their osier basket.

ALGON'S STRATEGY

Poor Algon returned home more unhappy than ever. All night he lay awake dreaming of the pretty, elusive creature who had wound a chain of gossamer round his heart and brain, and early in the morning he repaired to the enchanted spot. Casting about for some means of gaining his end, he came upon the hollow trunk of a tree in which a number of mice gambolled. With the aid of the charms in his "medicine"-bag he turned himself into one of these little animals, thinking the fair sisters would never pierce his disguise.

That day when the osier car descended its occupants alighted and danced merrily as they were wont in the magic circle, till the youngest saw the hollow tree-trunk (which had not been there on the previous day) and turned to fly. Her sisters laughed at her fears, and tried to reassure her by overturning the tree-trunk. The mice scampered in all directions, and were quickly pursued by the Star-maidens, who killed them all except Algon. The latter regained his own shape just as the youngest fairy raised her hand to strike him. Clasping her in his arms, he bore her to his village, while her frightened sisters ascended to their Star-country.

Arrived at his home, Algon married the maiden, and by his kindness and gentleness soon won her affection. However, her thoughts still dwelt on her own people, and though she indulged her sorrow only in secret, lest it should trouble her husband, she never ceased to lament her lost home.

THE STAR-MAIDEN'S ESCAPE

One day while she was out with her little son she made a basket of osiers, like the one in which she had first come to earth. Gathering together some flowers and gifts for the Star-people, she took the child with her into the basket, sang the magical songs she still remembered, and soon floated up to her own country, where she was welcomed by the king, her father.

Algon's grief was bitter indeed when he found that his wife and child had left him. But he had no means of following them. Every day he would go to the magic circle on the prairie and give vent to his sorrow, but the years went past and there was no sign of his dear ones returning.

Meanwhile the woman and her son had almost forgotten Algon and the earth-country. However, when the boy grew old enough to hear the story he wished to go and see his father. His mother consented, and arranged to go with him. While they were preparing to descend the Star-people said:

"Bring Algon with you when you return, and ask him to bring some feature from every beast and bird he has killed in the chase."

Algon, who had latterly spent almost all his time at the charmed circle, was overjoyed to see his wife and son come back to him, and willingly agreed to go with them to the Star-country. He worked very hard to obtain a specimen of all the rare and curious birds and beasts in his land, and when at last he had gathered the relics—a claw of one, a feather of another, and so on—he piled them in the osier car, climbed in himself with his wife and boy, and set off to the Star-country.

The people there were delighted with the curious gifts Algon had brought them, and, being permitted by their king to take one apiece, they did so. Those who took a tail or a claw of any beast at once became the quadruped represented by the fragment, and those who took the wings of birds became birds themselves. Algon and his wife and son took the feathers of a white falcon and flew down to the prairies, where their descendants may still be seen.

CLOUD-CARRIER AND THE STAR-FOLK

A handsome youth once dwelt with his parents on the banks of Lake Huron. The old people were very proud of their boy, and intended that he should become a great warrior. When he grew old enough to prepare

his "medicine"-bag he set off into the forest for that purpose. As he journeyed he grew weary, and lay down to sleep, and while he slept he heard
a gentle voice whisper:

"Cloud-carrier, I have come to fetch you. Follow me."

The young man started to his feet.

"I am dreaming. It is but an illusion," he muttered to himself, as he
gazed at the owner of the soft voice, who was a damsel of such marvelous
beauty that the sleepy eyes of Cloud-carrier were quite dazzled.

"Follow me," she said again, and rose softly from the ground like
thistledown. To his surprise the youth rose along with her, as lightly and as
easily. Higher they went, and still higher, far above the tree-tops, and into
the sky, till they passed at length through an opening in the spreading
vault, and Cloud-carrier saw that he was in the country of the Star-
people, and that his beautiful guide was no mortal maiden, but a supernatural being. So fascinated was he by her sweetness and gentleness that
he followed her without question till they came to a large lodge.
Entering it at the invitation of the Star-maiden, Cloud-carrier found it
filled with weapons and ornaments of silver, worked in strange and
grotesque designs. For a time he wandered through the lodge admiring
and praising all he saw, his warrior-blood stirring at the sight of the rare
weapons. Suddenly the lady cried:

"Hush! My brother approaches! Let me hide you. Quick!"

The young man crouched in a corner, and the damsel threw a richly
coloured scarf over him. Scarcely had she done so when a grave and dignified warrior stalked into the lodge.

"Nemissa, my dear sister," he said, after a moment's pause, "have you
not been forbidden to speak to the Earth-people? Perhaps you imagine
you have hidden the young man, but you have not." Then, turning from
the blushing Nemissa to Cloud-carrier, he added, good-naturedly:

"If you stay long there you will be very hungry. Come out and let us
have a talk."

The youth did as he was bid, and the brother of Nemissa gave him a
pipe and a bow and arrows. He gave him also Nemissa for his wife, and
for a long time they lived together very happily.

THE STAR-COUNTRY

Now the young man observed that his brother-in-law was in the habit
of going away every day by himself, and feeling curious to know what
his business might be, he asked one morning whether he might accompany him.

The brother-in-law consented readily, and the two set off. Travelling
in the Star-country was very pleasant. The foliage was richer than that of

the earth, the flowers more delicately coloured, the air softer and more fragrant, and the birds and beasts more graceful and harmless. As the day wore on to noon Cloud-carrier became very hungry.

"When can we get something to eat?" he asked his brother-in-law.

"Very soon," was the reassuring reply. "We are just going to make a repast." As he spoke they came to a large opening, through which they could see the lodges and lakes and forests of the earth. At one place some hunters were preparing for the chase. By the banks of a river some women were gathering reeds, and down in a village a number of children were playing happily.

"Do you see that boy down there in the centre of the group?" said the brother of Nemissa, and as he spoke he threw something at the child. The poor boy fell down instantly, and was carried, more dead than alive, to the nearest hut.

THE SACRIFICE

Cloud-carrier was much perplexed at the act of his supernatural relative. He saw the medicine-men gather round the child and chant prayers for his recovery.

"It is the will of Manitou," said one priest, "that we offer a white dog as a sacrifice."

So they procured a white dog, skinned and roasted it, and put it on a plate. It flew up in the air and provided a meal for the hungry Cloud-carrier and his companion. The child recovered and returned to his play.

"Your medicine-men," said Nemissa's brother, "get a great reputation for wisdom simply because they direct the people to me. You think they are very clever, but all they do is to advise you to sacrifice to me. It is I who recover the sick."

Cloud-carrier found in this spot a new source of interest, but at length the delights of the celestial regions began to pall. He longed for the companionship of his own kin, for the old commonplace pastimes of the Earth-country. He became, in short, very homesick, and begged his wife's permission to return to earth. Very reluctantly she consented.

"Remember," she said, "that I shall have the power to recall you when I please, for you will still be my husband. And above all do not marry an Earth-woman, or you will taste of my vengeance."

The young man readily promised to respect her injunctions. So he went to sleep, and awoke a little later to find himself lying on the grass close by his father's lodge. His parents greeted him joyfully. He had been absent, they told him, for more than a year, and they had not hoped to see him again.

The remembrance of his sojourn among the Star-people faded gradually to a dim recollection. By and by, forgetting the wife he had left there, he married a young and handsome woman belonging to his own village. Four days after the wedding she died, but Cloud-carrier failed to draw a lesson from this unfortunate occurrence. He married a third wife. But one day he was missing, and was never again heard of. His Star-wife had recalled him to the sky.

THE SNOW-MAN HUSBAND

In a northern village of the Algonquins dwelt a young girl so exquisitely beautiful that she attracted hosts of admirers. The fame of her beauty far and wide, and warriors and hunters thronged to her father's lodge in order to behold her. By universal consent she received the name of "Handsome." One of the braves who was most assiduous in paying her his addresses was surnamed "Elegant," because of the richness of his costume and the nobility of his features. Desiring to know his fate, the young man confided the secret of his love for Handsome to another of his suitors, and proposed that they two should that day approach her and ask her hand in marriage. But the coquettish maiden dismissed the young braves disdainfully, and, to add to the indignity of her refusal, repeated it in public outside her father's lodge. Elegant, who was extremely sensitive, was so humiliated and mortified that he fell into ill-health. A deep melancholy settled on his mind. He refused all nourishment, and for hours he would sit with his eyes fixed on the ground in moody contemplation. A profound sense of disgrace seized upon him, and notwithstanding the arguments of his relations and comrades he sank deeper into lethargy. Finally he took to his bed, and even when his family were preparing for the annual migration customary with the tribe he refused to rise from it, although they removed the tent from above his head and packed it up for transport.

THE LOVER'S REVENGE

After his family had gone Elegant appealed to his guardian spirit or totem to revenge him on the maiden who had thus cast him into despondency. Going from lodge to lodge, he collected all the rags that he could find, and, kneading snow over a framework of animals' bones, he moulded it into the shape of a man, which he attired in the tatters he had gathered, finally covering the whole with brilliant beads and gaudy feathers so that it presented a very imposing appearance. By magic art he animated this singular figure, placed a bow and arrows into its hands, and bestowed on it the name of Moowis.

Together the pair set out for the new encampment of the tribe. The brilliant appearance of Moowis caused him to be received by all with the most marked distinction. The chieftain of the tribe begged him to enter his lodge, and entertained him as an honoured guest. But none was so struck by the bearing of the noble-looking stranger as Handsome. Her mother requested him to accept the hospitality of her lodge, which he duly graced with his presence, but being unable to approach too closely to the hearth, on which a great fire was burning, he placed a boy between him and the blaze, in order that he should run no risk of melting. Soon the news that Moowis was to wed Handsome ran through the encampment, and the nuptials were celebrated. On the following day Moowis announced his intention of undertaking a long journey. Handsome pleaded for leave to accompany him, but he refused on the ground that the distance was too great and that the fatigues and dangers of the route would prove too much for her strength. Finally, however, she overcame his resistance, and the two set out.

A STRANGE TRANSFORMATION

A rough and rugged road had to be traversed by the newly wedded pair. On every hand they encountered obstacles, and the unfortunate Handsome, whose feet were cut and bleeding, found the greatest difficulty in keeping up with her more active husband. At first it was bitterly cold, but at length the sun came out and shone in all his strength, so that the girl forgot her woes and began to sing gaily. But on the appearance of the luminary a strange transformation had slowly overtaken her spouse. At first he attempted to keep in the shade, to avoid the golden beams that he knew meant death to him, but all to no purpose. The air became gradually warmer, and slowly he dissolved and fell to pieces, so that his frenzied wife now only beheld his garments, the bones that had composed his framework, and the gaudy plumes and beads with which he had been bedecked. Long she sought his real self, thinking that some trick had been played upon her; but at length, exhausted with fatigue and sorrow, she cast herself on the ground, and with his name on her lips breathed her last. So was Elegant avenged.

THE SPIRIT-BRIDE

A story is told of a young Algonquin brave whose bride died on the day fixed for their wedding. Before this sad event he had been the most courageous and high-spirited of warriors and the most skilful of hunters, but afterward his pride and his bravery seemed to desert him. In vain his friends urged him to seek the chase and begged him to take a greater interest in life. The more they pressed him the more melancholy he became, till at length he passed most of his time by the grave of his bride.

He was roused from his state of apathy one day, however, by hearing some old men discussing the existence of a path to the Spirit-world, which they supposed lay to the south. A gleam of hope shone in the young brave's breast, and, worn with sorrow as he was, he armed himself and set off southward. For a long time he saw no appreciable change in his surroundings—rivers, mountains, lakes, and forests similar to those of his own country environed him. But after a weary journey of many days he fancied he saw a difference. The sky was more blue, the prairie more fertile, the scenery more gloriously beautiful. From the conversation he had overheard before he set out, the young brave judged that he was nearing the Spirit-world. Just as he emerged from a spreading forest he saw before him a little lodge set high on a hill. Thinking its occupants might be able to direct him to this destination, he climbed to the lodge and accosted an aged man who stood in the doorway.

"Can you tell me the way to the Spirit-world?" he inquired.

THE ISLAND OF THE BLESSED

"Yes," said the old man gravely, throwing aside his cloak of swan's skin. "Only a few days ago she whom you seek rested in my lodge. If you will leave your body here you may follow her. To reach the Island of the Blessed you must cross yonder gulf you see in the distance. But I warn you the crossing will be no easy matter. Do you still wish to go?"

"Oh, yes, yes," cried the warrior eagerly, and as the words were uttered he felt himself grow suddenly lighter. The whole aspect, too, of the scene was changed. Everything looked brighter and more ethereal. He found himself in a moment walking through thickets which offered no resistance to his passage, and he knew that he was a spirit, travelling in the Spirit-world. When he reached the gulf which the old man had indicated he found to his delight a wonderful canoe ready on the shore. It was cut from a single white stone, and shone and sparkled in the sun like a jewel. The warrior lost no time in embarking, and as he put off from the shore he saw his pretty bride enter just such another canoe as his and imitate all his movements. Side by side they made for the Island of the Blessed, a charming woody islet set in the middle of the water, like an emerald in silver. When they were about halfway across a sudden storm arose, and the huge waves threatened to engulf them. Many other people had embarked on the perilous waters by this time, some of whom perished in the furious tempest. But the youth and maiden still battled on bravely, never losing sight of one another. Because they were good and innocent, the Master of Life had decreed that they should arrive safely at the fair island, and after a weary struggle they felt their canoes grate on the shore.

Hand in hand the lovers walked among the beautiful sights and sounds that greeted their eyes and ears from every quarter. There was no trace of the recent storm. The sea was as smooth as glass and the sky as clear as crystal. The youth and his bride felt that they could wander on thus forever. But at length a faint, sweet voice bade the former to return to this home in the Earth-country.

THE MASTER OF LIFE

"You must finish your mortal course," it whispered softly. "You will become a great chief among your own people. Rule wisely and well, and when your earthly career is over you shall return to your bride, who will retain her youth and beauty forever."

The young man recognized the voice as that of the Master of Life, and sadly bade farewell to the woman. He was not without hope now, however, but looked forward to another and more lasting reunion.

Returning to the old man's lodge, he regained his body, went home as the gentle voice on the island had commanded him, and became a father to his people for many years. By his just and kindly rule he won the hearts of all who knew him, and ensured for himself a safe passage to the Island of the Blessed, where he arrived at last to partake of everlasting happiness with his beautiful bride.

OTTER-HEART

In the heart of a great forest lay a nameless little lake, and by its side dwelt two children. Wicked magicians had slain their parents while they were yet of tender years, and the little orphans were obliged to fend for themselves. The younger of the two, a boy, learned to shoot with bow and arrow, and he soon acquired such skill that he rarely returned from a hunting expedition without a specimen of his prowess in the shape of a bird or a hare, which his elder sister would dress and cook.

When the boy grew older he naturally felt the need of some companionship other than that of his sister. During his long, solitary journeys in search of food he thought a good deal about the great world outside the barrier of the still, silent forest. He longed for the sound of human voices to replace the murmuring of the trees and the cries of the birds.

"Are there no Indians but ourselves in the whole world?" he would ask wistfully.

"I do not know," his sister invariably replied. Busying herself cheerfully about her household tasks, she knew nothing of the strange thoughts that were stirring in the mind of her brother.

But one day he returned from the chase in so discontented a mood that his unrest could no longer pass unnoticed. In response to solicitous inquiries from his sister, he said abruptly:

"Make me ten pairs of moccasins. Tomorrow I am going to travel into the great world."

The girl was much disturbed by this communication, but like a good Indian maiden she did as he requested her and kept a respectful silence.

Early on the following morning the youth, whose name was Otter-heart, set out on his quest. He soon came to a clearing in the forest, but to his disappointment he found that the tree-stumps were old and rotten.

"It is a long, long time," he said mournfully, "since there were Indians here."

In order that he might find his way back, he suspended a pair of moc-casins from the branch of a tree, and continued his journey. Other clearings he reached in due time, each showing traces of a more recent occupation than the last, but still it seemed to him that a long time must have elapsed since the trees were cut down, so he hung up a pair of moccasins at each stage of his journey, and pursued his course in search of human beings.

At last he saw before him an Indian village, which he approached with mingled feelings of pleasure and trepidation, natural enough when it is remembered that since his early childhood he had spoken to no one but his sister.

THE BALL-PLAYERS

On the outskirts of the village some youths of about his own age were engaged in a game of ball, in which they courteously invited the stranger to join. Very soon he had forgotten his natural shyness so far as to enter into the sport with whole-hearted zest and enjoyment. His new com-panions, for their part, were filled with astonishment at his skill and agility, and, wishing to do him honour, led him to the great lodge and introduced him to their chief.

Now the chief had two daughters, one of whom was surnamed "The Good" and the other "The Wicked." To the guest the names sounded rather suggestive, and he was not a little embarrassed when the chief begged him to marry the maidens.

"I will marry 'The Good,'" he declared.

But the chief would not agree to that.

"You must marry both," he said firmly.

Here was a dilemma for our hero, who had no wish to wed the cross, ugly sister. He tried hard to think of a way of escape.

"I am going to visit So-and-so," he said at last, mentioning the name of one of his companions at ball, and he dressed himself carefully as though he were about to pay a ceremonious visit.

Directly he was out of sight of the chief's lodge, however, he took to his heels and ran into the forest as hard as he could. Meanwhile the maidens sat waiting their intended bridegroom. When some hours passed without there being any signs of his coming they became alarmed, and set off to look for him.

Toward nightfall the young Otter-heart relaxed his speed. "I am quite safe now," he thought. He did not know that the sisters had the resources of magic at their command. Suddenly he heard wild laughter behind him. Recognizing the shrill voice of The Wicked, he knew that he was discovered, and cast about for a refuge. The only likely place was in the branches of a dense fir-tree, and almost as soon as the thought entered his mind he was at the top. His satisfaction was short-lived. In a moment the laughter of the women broke out anew, and they commenced to hew down the tree. But Otter-heart himself was not without some acquaintance with magic art. Plucking a small fir-cone from the tree-top, he threw it into the air, jumped astride it, and rode down the wind for half a mile or more. The sisters, absorbed in their task of cutting down the tree, did not notice that their bird was flown. When at last the great fir crashed to the ground and the youth was nowhere to be seen the pursuers tore their hair in rage and disappointment.

OTTER-HEART'S STRATAGEM

Only on the following evening did they overtake Otter-heart again. This time he had entered a hollow cedar-tree, the hard wood of which he thought would defy their axes. But he had underestimated the energy of the sisters. In a short time the tree showed the effect of their blows, and Otter-heart called on his guardian spirit to break one of the axes.

His wish was promptly gratified, but the other sister continued her labours with increased energy. Otter-heart now wished that the other axe might break, and again his desire was fulfilled. The sisters were at a loss to know what to do.

"We cannot take him by force," said one; "we must take him by subtlety. Let each do her best, and the one who gets him can keep him."

So they departed, and Otter-heart was free to emerge from his prison. He travelled another day's journey from the spot, and at last, reaching a place where he thought he would be safe, he laid down his blanket and went in search of food. Fortune favoured the hunter, and he shortly returned with a fine beaver. What was his amazement when he beheld a handsome lodge where he had left his blanket!

"It must be those women again," he muttered, preparing to fly. But the light shone so warmly from the lodge, and he was so tired and hungry, that he conquered his fears and entered. Within he found a tall, thin woman, pale and hungry-eyed, but rather pretty. Taking the beaver, she proceeded to cook it. As she did so Otter-heart noticed that she ate all the best parts herself, and when the meal was set out only the poorest pieces remained for him. This was so unlike an Indian housewife that he cast reproaches at her and accused her of greediness. As he spoke a curious change came over her. Her features grew longer and thinner. In a moment she had turned into a wolf and slunk into the forest. It was The Wicked, who had made herself pretty by means of magic, but could not conceal her voracious nature.

Otter-heart was glad to have found her out. He journeyed on still farther, laid down his blanket, and went to look for game. This time several beavers rewarded his skill, and he carried them to the place where he had left his blanket. Another handsome lodge had been erected there! More than ever he wanted to run away, but once more his hunger and fatigue detained him.

"Perhaps it is The Good," he said. "I shall go inside, and if she has laid my blanket near her couch I shall take it for a sign and she shall become my wife."

THE BEAVER-WOMAN

He entered the lodge, and found a small, pretty woman busily engaged in household duties. Sure enough she had laid his blanket near her couch. When she had dressed and cooked the beavers she gave the finest morsels to her husband, who was thoroughly pleased with his wife.

Hearing a sound in the night, Otter-heart awoke, and fancied he saw his wife chewing birch-bark. When he told her of the dream in the morning she did not laugh, but looked very serious.

"Tell me," asked Otter-heart, "why did you examine the beavers so closely yesterday?"

"They were my relatives," she replied; "my cousin, my aunt, and my great-uncle."

Otter-heart was more than ever delighted, for the otters, his totem-kin, and the beavers had always been on very good terms. He promised never to kill any more beavers, but only deer and birds, and he and his wife, The Good, lived together very happily for a long time.

THE FAIRY WIVES

Once upon a time there dwelt in the forest two braves, one of whom was called the Moose and the other the Marten. Moose was a great hunter, and never returned from the chase without a fine deer or buffalo, which he would give to his old grandmother to prepare for cooking. Marten, on the other hand, was an idler, and never hunted at all if he could obtain food by any other means. When Moose brought home a trophy of his skill in the hunt Marten would repair to his friend's lodge and beg for a portion of the meat. Being a good-natured fellow, Moose generally gave him what he asked for, to the indignation of the old grandmother, who declared that the lazy creature had much better learn to work for himself.

"Do not encourage his idle habits," said she to her grandson. "If you stop giving him food he will go and hunt for himself."

Moose agreed with the old woman, and having on his next expedition killed a bear, he told the grandmother to hide it, so that Marten might know nothing of it.

When the time came to cook the bear-meat, however, the grandmother found that her kettle would not hold water, and remembering that Marten had just got a nice new kettle, she went to borrow his.

"I will clean it well before I return it," she thought. "He will never know what I want it for."

But Marten made a very good guess, so he laid a spell on the kettle before lending it, and afterward set out for Moose's lodge. Looking in, he beheld a great quantity of bear-meat.

"I shall have a fine feast tomorrow," said he, laughing, as he stole quietly away without being seen.

On the following day the old grandmother of Moose took the borrowed kettle, cleaned it carefully, and carried it to its owner. She never dreamed that he would suspect anything.

"Oh," said Marten, "what a fine kettleful of bear-meat you have brought me!"

"I have brought you nothing," the old woman began in astonishment, but a glance at her kettle showed her that it was full of steaming bear-meat. She was much confused, and knew that Marten had discovered her plot by magic art.

MOOSE DEMANDS A WIFE

Though Marten was by no means so brave or so industrious as Moose, he nevertheless had two very beautiful wives, while his companion had not even one. Moose thought this rather unfair, so he ventured to ask Marten for one of his wives. To this Marten would not agree, nor would either of the women consent to be handed over to Moose, so there was nothing for it but that the braves should fight for the wives, who, all unknown to their husband, were fairies. And fight they did, that day and the next and the next, till it grew to be a habit with them, and they fought as regularly as they slept.

In the morning Moose would say: "Give me one of your wives." "Paddle your own canoe," Marten would retort, and the fight would begin. Next morning Moose would say again: "Give me one of your wives." "Fish for your own minnows," the reply would come, and the quarrel would be continued with tomahawks for arguments.

"Give me one of your wives," Moose persisted.

"Skin your own rabbits!"

Meanwhile the wives of Marten had grown tired of the perpetual skirmishing. So they made up their minds to run away. Moose and Marten never missed them: they were too busy fighting.

All day the fairy wives, whose name was Weasel, travelled as fast as they could, for they did not want to be caught. But when night came they lay down on the banks of a stream and watched the stars shining through the pine-branches.

"If you were a Star-maiden," said one, "and wished to marry a star, which one would you chose?"

"I would marry that bright little red one," said the other. "I am sure he must be a merry little fellow."

"I," said her companion, "should like to marry that big yellow one. I think he must be a great warrior." And so saying she fell asleep.

THE RED STAR AND THE YELLOW STAR

When they awoke in the morning the fairies found that their wishes were fulfilled. One was the wife of the great yellow star, and the other the wife of the little red one.

This was the work of an Indian spirit, whose duty it is to punish unfaithful wives, and who had overheard their remarks on the previous night. Knowing that the fulfilment of their wishes would be the best punishment, he transported them to the Star-country, where they were wedded to the stars of their choice. And punishment it was, for the Yellow Star was a fierce warrior who frightened his wife nearly out of her wits, and the Red Star was an irritable old man, and his wife was obliged to wait on him hand and foot. Before very long the fairies found their life in the Star-country exceedingly irksome, and they wished they had never quitted their home.

Not far from their lodges was a large white stone, which their husbands had forbidden them to touch, but which their curiosity one day tempted them to remove. Far below they saw the Earth-country, and they became sadder and more homesick than ever. The Star-husbands, whose magic powers told them that their wives had been disobedient, were not really cruel or unkind at heart, so they decided to let the fairies return to earth.

"We do not want wives who will not obey," they said, "so you may go to your own country if you will be obedient once."

The fairies joyfully promised to do whatever was required of them if they might return home.

"Very well," the stars replied. "You must sleep tonight, and in the morning you will wake and hear the song of the chickadee, but do not open your eyes. Then you will hear the voice of the ground-squirrel; still you must not rise. The red squirrel also you shall hear, but the success of our scheme depends on your remaining quiet. Only when you hear the striped squirrel you may get up."

THE RETURN TO EARTH

The fairies went to their couch and slept, but their sleep was broken by impatience. In the morning the chickadee woke them with its song. The younger fairy eagerly started up, but the other drew her back.

"Let us wait till we hear the striped squirrel," said she.

When the red squirrel's note was heard the younger fairy could no longer curb her impatience. She sprang to her feet, dragging her companion with her. They had indeed reached the Earth-country, but in a way that helped them but little, for they found themselves in the topmost branches of the highest tree in the forest, with no prospect of getting down. In vain they called to the birds and animals to help them; all the creatures were too busy to pay any attention to their plight. At last Lox, the wolverine, passed under the tree, and though he was the wickedest of the animals the Weasels cried to him for help.

"If you will promise to come to my lodge," said Lox, "I will help you."

"We will build lodges for you," cried the elder fairy, who had been thinking of a way of escape.

"That is well," said Lox; "I will take you down."

While he was descending the tree with the younger of the fairies the elder one wound her magic hair-string in the branches, knotting it skilfully, so that the task of undoing it would be no light one. When she in her turn had been carried to the ground she begged Lox to return for her hair-string, which, she said, had become entangled among the branches.

"Pray do not break it," she added, "for if you do I shall have no good fortune."

THE ESCAPE FROM LOX

Once more Lox ascended the tall pine, and strove with the knots which the cunning fairy had tied. Meanwhile the Weasels built him a wigwam. They filled it with thorns and briers and all sorts of prickly things, and induced their friends the ants and hornets to make their nests inside. So long did Lox take to untie the knotted hair-string that when he came down it was quite dark. He was in a very bad temper, and pushed his way angrily into the new lodge. All the little creatures attacked him instantly, the ants bit him, the thorns pricked him, so that he cried out with anger and pain.

The fairies ran away as fast as they could, and by and by found them-

selves on the brink of a wide river. The younger sat down and began to
weep, thinking that Lox would certainly overtake them. But the elder
was more resourceful. She saw the Crane, who was ferryman, standing
close by, and sang a very sweet song in praise of his long legs and soft
feathers.

"Will you carry us over the river?" she asked at length.

"Willingly," replied the Crane, who was very susceptible to flattery,
and he ferried them across the river.

They were just in time. Scarcely had they reached the opposite bank
when Lox appeared on the scene, very angry and out of breath.

"Ferry me across, Old Crooked-legs," said he, and added other still
more uncomplimentary remarks.

The Crane was furious, but he said nothing, and bore Lox out on the
river.

"I see you," cried Lox to the trembling fairies. "I shall have you soon!"

"You shall not, wicked one," said the Crane, and he threw Lox into
the deepest part of the stream.

The fairies turned their faces homeward and saw him no more.

THE MALICIOUS MOTHER-IN-LAW

An Ojibway or Chippeway legend tells of a hunter who was greatly
devoted to his wife. As a proof of his affection he presented her with the
most delicate morsels from the game he killed. This aroused the jealousy
and envy of his mother, who lived with them, and who imagined that
these little attentions should be paid to her, and not to the younger
woman. The latter, quite unaware of her mother-in-law's attitude,
cooked and ate the gifts her husband brought her. Being a woman of a
gentle and agreeable disposition, who spent most of her time attending
to her household duties and watching over her child and a little orphan
boy whom she had adopted, she tried to make friends with the old dame,
and was grieved and disappointed when the latter would not respond to
her advances.

The mother-in-law nursed her grievance until it seemed of gigantic
proportions. Her heart grew blacker and blacker against her son's wife,
and at last she determined to kill her. For a time she could think of no
way to put her evil intent into action, but finally she hit upon a plan.

One day she disappeared from the lodge, and returned after a space
looking very happy and good-tempered. The younger woman was surprised and delighted at the alteration. This was an agreeably different
person from the nagging, cross-grained old creature who had made her
life a burden! The old woman repeatedly absented herself from her home
after this, returning on each occasion with a pleased and contented smile
on her wrinkled face. By and by the wife allowed her curiosity to get the

better of her, and she asked the meaning of her mother-in-law's happiness.

THE DEATH-SWING

"If you must know," replied the old woman, "I have made a beautiful swing down by the lake, and always when I swing on it I feel so well and happy that I cannot help smiling."

The young woman begged that she too might be allowed to enjoy the swing.

"Tomorrow you may accompany me," was the reply. But next day the old woman had some excuse, and so on, day after day, till the curiosity of her son's wife was very keen. Thus when the elder woman said one day, "Come with me, and I will take you to the swing. Tie up your baby and leave him in charge of the orphan," the other complied eagerly, and was ready in a moment to go with her mother-in-law.

When they reached the shores of the lake they found a lithe sapling which hung over the water.

"Here is my swing," said the old creature, and she cast aside her robe, fastened a thong to her waist and to the sapling, and swung far over the lake. She laughed so much and seemed to find the pastime so pleasant that her daughter-in-law was more anxious than ever to try it for herself.

"Let me tie the thong for you," said the old woman, when she had tired of swinging. Her companion threw off her robe and allowed the leather thong to be fastened round her waist. When all was ready she was commanded to swing. Out over the water she went fearlessly, but as she did so the jealous old mother-in-law cut the thong, and she fell into the lake.

The old creature, exulting over the success of her cruel scheme, dressed herself in her victim's clothes and returned to the lodge. But the baby cried and refused to be fed by her, and the orphan boy cried too, for the young woman had been almost a mother to him since his parents had died.

"Where is the baby's mother?" he asked, when some hours had passed and she did not return.

"At the swing," replied the old woman roughly.

When the hunter returned from the chase he brought with him, as usual, some morsels of game for his wife, and, never dreaming that the woman bending over the child might not be she, he gave them to her. The lodge was dark, for it was evening, and his mother wore the clothes of his wife and imitated her voice and movements, so that his error was not surprising. Greedily she seized the tender pieces of meat, and cooked and ate them.

The heart of the little orphan was so sore that he could not sleep. In the middle of the night he rose and went to look for his foster-mother. Down by the lake he found the swing with the thong cut, and he knew that she had been killed. Crying bitterly, he crept home to his couch, and in the morning told the hunter all that he had seen.

"Say nothing," said the chief, "but come with me to hunt, and in the evening return to the shores of the lake with the child, while I pray to Manitou that he may send me back my wife."

THE SILVER GIRDLE

So they went off in search of game without a word to the old woman; nor did they stay to eat, but set out directly when it was light. At sunset they made their way to the lake-side, the little orphan carrying the baby. Here the hunter blackened his face and prayed earnestly that the Great Manitou might send back his wife. While he prayed the orphan amused the child by singing quaint little songs; but at last the baby grew weary and hungry and began to cry.

Far in the lake his mother heard the sound, and skimmed over the water in the shape of a great white gull. When she touched the shore she became a woman again, and hugged the child to her heart's content. The orphan boy besought her to return to them.

"Alas!" said she, "I have fallen into the hands of the Water Manitou, and he has wound his silver tail about me, so that I never can escape."

As she spoke the little lad saw that her waist was encircled by a band of gleaming silver, one end of which was in the water. At length she declared that it was time for her to return to the home of the water-god, and after having exacted a promise from the boy that he would bring her baby there every day, she became a gull again and flew away. The hunter was informed of all that had passed, and straightaway determined that he would be present on the following evening. All next day he fasted and besought the good-will of Manitou, and when the night began to fall he hid himself on the shore till his wife appeared. Hastily emerging from his concealment, the hunter poised his spear and struck the girdle with all his force. The silver band parted, and the woman was free to return home with her husband.

Overjoyed at her restoration, he led her gently to the lodge, where his mother was sitting by the fire. At the sight of her daughter-in-law, whom she thought she had drowned in the lake, she started up in such fear and astonishment that she tripped, overbalanced, and fell into a fire. Before they could pull her out the flames had risen to the smoke-hole, and when the fire died down no woman was there, but a great black bird, which rose slowly from the smoking embers, flew out of the lodge, and was never seen again.

As for the others, they lived long and happily, undisturbed by the jealousy and hatred of the malicious crone.

THE MAIZE SPIRIT

The Chippeways tell a charming story concerning the origin of the zea maize, which runs as follows:

A lad of fourteen or fifteen dwelt with his parents, brothers, and sisters in a beautifully situated little lodge. The family, though poor, were very happy and contented. The father was a hunter who was not lacking in courage and skill, but there were times when he could scarcely supply the wants of his family, and as none of his children was old enough to help him things went hardly with them then. The lad was of a cheerful and contented disposition, like his father, and his great desire was to benefit his people. The time had come for him to observe the initial fast prescribed for all Indian boys of his age, and his mother made him a little fasting-lodge in a remote spot where he might not suffer interruption during his ordeal.

Thither the boy repaired, meditating on the goodness of the Great Spirit, who had made all things beautiful in the fields and forests for the enjoyment of man. The desire to help his fellows was strong upon him, and he prayed that some means to that end might be revealed to him in a dream.

On the third day of his fast he was too weak to ramble through the forest, and as he lay in a state between sleeping and waking there came toward him a beautiful youth, richly dressed in green robes, and wearing on his head wonderful green plumes.

"The Great Spirit has heard your prayers," said the youth, and his voice was like the sound of the wind sighing through the grass. "Hearken to me and you shall have your desire fulfilled. Arise and wrestle with me."

THE STRUGGLE

The lad obeyed. Though his limbs were weak his brain was clear and active, and he felt he could not but obey the soft-voiced stranger. After a long, silent struggle the latter said:

"That will do for today. Tomorrow I shall come again."

The lad lay back exhausted, but on the morrow the green-clad stranger reappeared, and the conflict was renewed. As the struggle went on the youth felt himself grow stronger and more confident, and before leaving him for the second time the supernatural visitor offered him some words of praise and encouragement.

On the third day the youth, pale and feeble, was again summoned to the contest. As he grasped his opponent the very contact seemed to give him new strength, and he fought more and more bravely, till his lithe companion was forced to cry out that he had had enough. Ere he took his departure the visitor told the lad that the following day would put an end to his trials.

"Tomorrow," said he, "your father will bring you food, and that will help you. In the evening I shall come and wrestle with you. I know that you are destined to succeed and to obtain your heart's desire. When you have thrown me, strip off my garments and plumes, bury me where I fall, and keep the earth above me moist and clean. Once a month let my remains be covered with fresh earth, and you shall see me again, clothed in my green garments and plumes." So saying, he vanished.

THE FINAL CONTEST

Next day the lad's father brought him food; the youth, however, begged that it might be set aside till evening. Once again the stranger appeared. Though he had eaten nothing, the hero's strength, as before, seemed to increase as he struggled, and at length he threw his opponent. Then he stripped off his garments and plumes, and buried him in the earth, not without sorrow in his heart for the slaying of such a beautiful youth.

His task done, he returned to his parents, and soon recovered his full strength. But he never forgot the grave of his friend. Not a weed was allowed to grow on it, and finally he was rewarded by seeing the green plumes rise above the earth and broaden out into graceful leaves. When the autumn came he requested his father to accompany him to the place. By this time the plant was at its full height, tall and beautiful, with waving leaves and golden tassels. The elder man was filled with surprise and admiration.

"It is my friend," murmured the youth, "the friend of my dreams."

"It is Mon-da-min," said his father, "the spirit's grain, the gift of the Great Spirit."

And in this manner was maize given to the Indians.

THE SEVEN BROTHERS

The Blackfeet have a curious legend in explanation of the constellation known as the Plough or Great Bear. Once there dwelt together nine children, seven boys and two girls. While the six older brothers were away on the warpath the elder daughter, whose name was Bearskin-woman, married a grizzly bear. Her father was so enraged that he collected his friends and ordered them to surround the grizzly's cave and slay him. When the girl heard that her spouse had been killed she took a piece of his skin and wore it as an amulet. Through the agency of her husband's supernatural power, one dark night she was changed into a grizzly bear, and rushed through the camp, killing and rending the people, even her own father and mother, sparing only her youngest brother and her sister,

Okinai and Sinopa. She then took her former shape, and returned to the lodge occupied by the two orphans, who were greatly terrified when they heard her muttering to herself, planning their deaths.

Sinopa had gone to the river one day, when she met her six brothers returning from the warpath. She told them what had happened in their absence. They reassured her, and bade her gather a large number of prickly pears. These she was to strew in front of the lodge, leaving only a small path uncovered by them. In the dead of night Okinai and Sinopa crept out of the lodge, picking their way down the little path that was free from the prickly pears, and meeting their six brothers, who were awaiting them. The Bearskin-woman heard them leaving the lodge, and rushed out into the open, only to tread on the prickly pears. Roaring with pain and anger, she immediately assumed her bear shape and rushed furiously at her brothers. But Okinai rose to the occasion. He shot an arrow into the air, and so far as it flew the brothers and sister found themselves just that distance in front of the savage animal behind them.

THE CHASE

The beast gained on them, however; but Okinai waved a magic feather, and thick underbrush rose in its path. Again Bearskin-woman made headway. Okinai caused a lake to spring up before her. Yet again she neared the brothers and sister, and this time Okinai raised a great tree, into which the refugees climbed. The Grizzly-woman, however, succeeded in dragging four of the brothers from the tree, when Okinai shot an arrow into the air. Immediately his little sister sailed into the sky. Six times more he shot an arrow, and each time a brother went up, Okinai himself following them as the last arrow soared into the blue. Thus the orphans became stars; and one can see that they took the same position in the sky as they had occupied in the tree, for the small star at one side of the bunch is Sinopa, while the four who huddle together at the bottom are those who had been dragged from the branches by Bearskin-woman.

THE BEAVER MEDICINE LEGEND[2]

Two brothers dwelt together in the old time. The elder, who was named Nopatsis, was married to a woman who was wholly evil, and who hated his younger brother, Akaiyan. Daily the wife pestered her husband to be rid of Akaiyan, but he would not agree to part with his only brother, for

---

[2] The first portion of this legend has its exact counterpart in Egyptian story. See Wiedemann, *Popular Literature of Ancient Egypt*, p. 45.

they had been together through long years of privation—indeed, since their parents had left them together as little helpless orphans—and they were all in all to each other. So the wife of Nopatsis had to resort to a ruse well known to women whose hearts are evil. One day when her husband returned from the chase he found her lamenting with torn clothes and disordered appearance. She told him that Akaiyan had treated her brutally. The lie entered into the heart of Nopatsis and made it heavy, so that in time he conceived a hatred of his innocent brother, and debated with himself how he should rid himself of Akaiyan.

Summer arrived, and with it the moulting season when the wild waterfowl shed their feathers, with which the Indians fledge their arrows. Near Nopatsis's lodge there was a great lake, to which these birds resorted in large numbers, and to this place the brothers went to collect feathers with which to plume their darts. They built a raft to enable them to reach an island in the middle of the lake, making it of logs bound securely with buffalo-hide. Embarking, they sailed to the little island, along the shores of which they walked, looking for suitable feathers. They parted in the quest, and after some time Akaiyan, who had wandered far along the strand, suddenly looked up to see his brother on the raft sailing toward the mainland. He called loudly to him to return, but Nopatsis replied that he deserved to perish there because of the brutal manner in which he had treated his sister-in-law. Akaiyan solemnly swore that he had not injured her in any way, but Nopatsis only jeered at him, and rowed away. Soon he was lost to sight, and Akaiyan sat down and wept bitterly. He prayed earnestly to the nature spirits and to the sun and moon, after which he felt greatly uplifted. Then he improvised a shelter of branches, and made a bed of feathers of the most comfortable description. He lived well on the ducks and geese which frequented the island, and made a warm robe against the winter season from their skins. He was careful also to preserve many of the tame birds for his winter food.

One day he encountered the lodge of a beaver, and while he looked at it curiously he became aware of the presence of a little beaver.

"My father desires that you will enter his dwelling," said the animal. So Akaiyan accepted the invitation and entered the lodge, where the Great Beaver, attended by his wife and family, received him. He was, indeed, the chief of all the beavers, and white with the snows of count-less winters. Akaiyan told the Beaver how cruelly he had been treated, and the wise animal condoled with him, and invited him to spend the winter in his lodge, when he would learn many wonderful and useful things. Akaiyan gratefully accepted the invitation, and when the beavers closed up their lodge for the winter he remained with them. They kept him warm by placing their thick, soft tails on his body, and taught him the secret of the healing art, the use of tobacco, and various ceremonial dances, songs, and prayers belonging to the great mystery of "medicine."

The summer returned, and on parting the Beaver asked Akaiyan to choose a gift. He chose the Beaver's youngest child, with whom he had contracted a strong friendship; but the father prized his little one greatly, and would not at first permit him to go. At length, however, Great Beaver gave way to Akaiyan's entreaties and allowed him to take Little Beaver with him, counselling him to construct a sacred Beaver Bundle when he arrived at his native village.

In due time Nopatsis came to the island on his raft, and, making sure that his brother was dead, began to search for his remains. But while he searched, Akaiyan caught up Little Beaver in his arms and, embarking on the raft, made for the mainland, espied by Nopatsis. When Akaiyan arrived at his native village he told his story to the chief, gathered a Beaver Bundle, and commenced to teach the people the mystery of "medicine," with its accompanying songs and dances. Then he invited the chiefs of the animal tribes to contribute their knowledge to the Beaver Medicine, which many of them did.

Having accomplished his task of instruction, which occupied him all winter, Akaiyan returned to the island with Little Beaver, who had been of immense service to him in teaching the Indians the "medicine" songs and dances. He returned Little Beaver to his parents, and received in exchange for him a sacred pipe, being also instructed in its accompanying songs and ceremonial dances. On the island he found the bones of his credulous and vengeful brother, who had met with the fate he had purposed for the innocent Akaiyan. Every spring Akaiyan visited the beavers, and as regularly he received something to add to the Beaver Medicine Bundle, until it reached the great size it now has. And he married and founded a race of medicine-men who have handed down the traditions and ceremonials of the Beaver Medicine to the present day.

THE SACRED BEAR-SPEAR

An interesting Blackfoot myth relates how that tribe obtained its sacred Bear-spear. Many generations ago, even before the Blackfeet used horses as beasts of burden, the tribe was undertaking its autumn migration, when one evening before striking camp for the night it was reported that a dog-sledge or cart belonging to the chief was missing. To make matters worse, the chief's ermine robe and his wife's buckskin dress, with her sacred elk-skin robe, had been packed in the little cart. Strangely enough, no one could recollect having noticed the dog during the march. Messengers were dispatched to the camping-site of the night before, but to no avail. At last the chief's son, Sokumapi, a boy about twelve years of age, begged to be allowed to search for the missing dog, a proposal to which his father, after some demur, consented. Sokumapi set out alone for the last camping-ground, which was under the shadows of the Rocky Mountains, and carefully examined the site. Soon he found a single dog-sledge track leading into a deep gulch, near the entrance to which he discovered a large cave. A heap of freshly turned earth stood in front of the cave, beside which was the missing cart. As he stood looking at it, wondering what had become of the dog which had drawn it, an immense grizzly bear suddenly dashed out. So rapid was its attack that Sokumapi had no chance either to defend himself or to take refuge in flight. The bear, giving vent to the most terrific roars, dragged him into the cave, hugging him with such force that he fainted. When he regained consciousness it was to find the bear's great head within a foot of his own, and he thought that he saw a kindly and almost human expression in its big brown eyes. For a long time he lay still, until at last, to his intense surprise, the Bear broke the silence by addressing him in human speech.

"Have no fear," said the grizzly. "I am the Great Bear, and my power is extensive. I know the circumstances of your search, and I have drawn you to this cavern because I desired to assist you. Winter is upon us, and you had better remain with me during the cold season, in the course of which I will reveal to you the secret of my supernatural power."

BEAR MAGIC

It will be observed that the circumstances of this tale are almost identical with those which relate to the manner in which the Beaver Medicine was revealed to mankind. The hero of both stories remains during the winter with the animal, the chief of its species, who in the period of hibernation instructs him in certain potent mysteries.

The Bear, having reassured Sokumapi, showed him how to transform various substances into food. His strange host slept during most of the winter; but when the warm winds of spring returned and the snows melted from the hills the grizzly became restless, and told Sokumapi that it was time to leave the cave. Before they quitted it, however, he taught the lad the secret of his supernatural power. Among other things, he showed him how to make a Bear-spear. He instructed him to take a long stick, to one end of which he must secure a sharp point, to symbolize the bear's tusks. To the staff must be attached a bear's nose and teeth, while the rest of the spear was to be covered with bear's skin, painted the sacred colour, red. The Bear also told him to decorate the handle with eagle's feathers and grizzly claws, and in wartime to wear a grizzly claw in his hair, so that the strength of the Great Bear might go with him in battle, and to imitate the noise a grizzly makes when it charges. The Bear furthermore instructed him what songs should be used in order to heal the sick, and how to paint his face and body so that he would be invulnerable in battle, and, lastly, told him of the sacred nature of the spear, which was only to be employed in warfare and for curing disease. Thus if a person was sick unto death, and a relative purchased the Bear-spear, its supernatural power would restore the ailing man to health. Equipped with this knowledge, Sokumapi returned to his people, who had long mourned him as dead. After a feast had been given to celebrate his home coming he began to manufacture the Bear-spear as directed by his friend.

HOW THE MAGIC WORKED

Shortly after his return the Crows made war upon the Blackfeet, and on the meeting of the two tribes in battle Sokumapi appeared in front of his people carrying the Bear-spear on his back. His face and body were painted as the Great Bear had instructed him, and he sang the battle-songs that the grizzly had taught him. After these ceremonies he impetuously charged the enemy, followed by all his braves in a solid phalanx, and such was the efficacy of the Bear magic that the Crows immediately took flight. The victorious Blackfeet brought back Sokumapi to their camp in triumph, to the accompaniment of the Bear songs. He was made a war-chief, and ever afterward the spear which he had used was regarded as the palladium of the Blackfoot Indians. In the spring the Bear-spear is unrolled from its covering and produced when the first thunder is heard, and when the Bear begins to quit his winter quarters; but when the Bear returns to his den to hibernate the spear is once more rolled up and put away. The greatest care is taken to protect it against injury. It has a special guardian, and no woman is permitted to touch it.

THE YOUNG DOG DANCE

A dance resembling the Sun Dance was formerly known to the Pawnee Indians, who called it the Young Dog Dance. It was, they said, borrowed from the Crees, who produced the following myth to account for it.

One day a young brave of the Cree tribe had gone out from his village to catch eagles, in order to provide himself with feathers for a war-bonnet, or to tie in his hair. Now the Crees caught eagles in this fashion. On the top of a hill frequented by these birds they would dig a pit and cover it over with a roof of poles, cunningly concealing the structure with grass. A piece of meat was fastened to the poles, so that the eagles could not carry it off. Then the Indian, taking off his clothes, would descend into the pit, and remain there for hours, or days, as the case may be, until an eagle was attracted by the bait, when he would put his hand between the poles, seize the bird by the feet, and quickly dispatch it.

The young brave whose fortune it was to discover the Young Dog

Dance had prepared the trap in this wise, and was lying in the pit praying that an eagle might come and bring his uncomfortable vigil to an end. Suddenly he heard a sound of drumming, distant but quite distinct, though he could not tell from what direction it proceeded. All night the mysterious noise continued. Next night as he lay in the same position he heard it again, and resolved to find out its origin, so he clambered out of his pit and went off in the direction from which the drumbeating seemed to proceed. At last, when dawn was near, he reached the shores of a great lake. Here he stopped, for the sounds quite evidently came from the lake. All that day he sat by the water bemoaning his ill-luck and praying for better fortune. When night fell the drumming began anew, and the young man saw countless animals and birds swimming in the lake. Four days he remained on the lakeshore, till at length, worn out by fatigue and hunger (for many days had elapsed since he had eaten), he fell asleep.

THE LODGE OF ANIMALS

When he awoke he found himself in a large lodge, surrounded by many people, some of whom were dancing, while others sat round the walls. All these people wore robes made from the skins of voracious animals or birds. They were, in fact, the animals the young Indian had seen swimming in the water, who had changed themselves into human shape. A chief at the back of the lodge stood up and addressed him thus:

"My friend, we have heard your prayers, and our desire is to help you. You see these people? They represent the animals. I am the Dog. The Great Spirit is very fond of dogs. I have much power, and my power I shall give to you, so that you may be like me, and my spirit will always protect you. Take this dance home to your people, and it will make them lucky in war." And he imparted the nature of the rite to the Indian by action.

The Dog turned from the Cree brave and his eye swept the company.

THE GIFT

"Brothers," he said, "I have given him my power. Will you not pity him and give him the power you have?"

For a time there was silence. No one seemed disposed to respond to the chief's appeal. At last the Owl rose.

"I will help you," he said to the young man. "I have power to see in the dark wherever I may go. When you go out at night I will be near you, and you shall see as well as I do. Take these feathers and tie them in your hair." And, giving him a bunch of feathers, the Owl sat down.

There was a pause, and the next to rise was the Buffalo Bull, who gave to the young Indian his strength and endurance and the power to trample his enemies underfoot. As a token he gave him a shoulder-belt of tanned buffalo-hide, bidding him wear it when he went on the warpath.

By and by the Porcupine stood up and addressed the guest. Giving him some of his quills with which to ornament the leather belt, he said: "I also will help you. I can make my enemies as weak as women, so that they fly before me. When you fight your foes shall flee and you shall overcome them."

Another long silence ensued, and when at last the Eagle rose everyone listened to hear what he had to say.

"I also," he said majestically, "will be with you wherever you go, and will give you my prowess in war, so that you may kill your foes as I do." As he spoke he handed to the brave some eagle feathers to tie in his hair.

The Whoopping Crane followed, and gave him a bone from its wing for a war-whistle to frighten his enemies away.

The Deer and the Bear came next, the one giving him swiftness, with a rattle as token, and the other hardiness, and a strip of fur for his belt.

After he had received these gifts from the animals the brave lay down and fell asleep again. When he awoke he found himself on the shores of the lake once more.

Returning home, he taught the Crees the Young Dog Dance, which was to make them skilful in war, and showed them the articles he had received. So the young men formed a Society of Young Dogs, which practised the dance and obtained the benefits.

THE MEDICINE WOLF

A quaint story of a "medicine" wolf is told among the Blackfoot Indians. On one occasion when the Blackfeet were moving camp they were attacked by a number of Crow Indians who had been lying in wait for them. The Blackfeet were travelling slowly in a long, straggling line, with the old men and the women and children in the middle, and a band of warriors in front and in the rear. The Crows, as has been said, made an ambush for their enemies, and rushed out on the middle portion of the line. Before either party of the Blackfoot warriors could reach the scene of the struggle many of the women and children had perished, and others were taken captive by the attacking force. Among the prisoners was a young woman called Sits-by-the-door. Many weary miles lay between them and the Crow camp on the Yellowstone River, but at length the tired captives, mounted with their captors on jaded horses, arrived at their destination. The warrior who had taken Sits-by-the-door prisoner now presented her to a friend of his, who in turn gave her into the keeping of his wife, who was somewhat older than her charge. The young Blackfoot woman was cruelly treated by the Crow into whose possession she had passed. Every night he tied her feet together so that she might not escape, and also tied a rope round her waist, the other end of which he fastened to his wife. The Crow woman, however, was not unmoved by the wretchedness of her prisoner. While her husband was out she managed to converse with her and to show her that she pitied her misfortunes. One day she informed Sits-by-the-door that she had overheard her husband and his companions plotting to kill her, but she added that when darkness fell she would help her to escape. When night came the Crow woman waited until the deep breathing of her husband told her that he was sound asleep; then, rising cautiously, she loosened the ropes that bound her captive, and, giving her a pair of moccasins, a flint, and a small sack of pemmican, bade her make haste and escape from the fate that would surely befall her if she remained where she was. The trembling woman obeyed, and travelled at a good pace all night. At dawn she hid in the dense undergrowth, hoping to escape observation should her captors pursue her. They, meanwhile, had discovered her absence, and were searching high and low, but no tracks were visible, and at last, wearied with their unprofitable search, they gave up the chase and returned to their homes.

THE FRIENDLY WOLF

When the woman had journeyed on for four nights she stopped concealing herself in the daytime and travelled straight on. She was not yet out of danger, however, for her supply of pemmican was soon exhausted, and she found herself face to face with the miseries of starvation. Her moccasins, besides, were worn to holes and her feet were cut and bleeding, while, to add to her misfortunes, a huge wolf dogged her every movement. In vain she tried to run away; her strength was exhausted and she sank to the ground. Nearer and nearer came the great wolf, and at last he lay down at her feet. Whenever the woman walked on her way the wolf followed, and when she lay down to rest he lay down also.

At length she begged her strange companion to help her, for she knew that unless she obtained food very soon she must die. The animal trotted away, and returned shortly with a buffalo calf which it had killed, and laid it at the woman's feet. With the aid of the flint—one of the gifts with which the Crow woman had sped her unhappy guest—she built a fire and cooked some of the buffalo meat. Thus refreshed, she proceeded on her way. Again and again the wolf provided food in a similar manner, until at length they reached the Blackfoot camp. The woman led the animal into her lodge, and related to her friends all that had befallen her in the Crow camp, and the manner of her escape. She also told them how the wolf had befriended her, and begged them to treat it kindly. But soon afterward she fell ill, and the poor wolf was driven out of the village by the Indian dogs. Every evening he would come to the top of the hill overlooking the camp and watch the lodge were Sits-by-the-door dwelt. Though he was still fed by her friends, after a time he disappeared and was seen no more.[3]

THE STORY OF SCAR-FACE

Scar-face was brave but poor. His parents had died while he was yet a boy, and he had no near relations. But his heart was high, and he was a mighty hunter. The old men said that Scar-face had a future before him, but the young braves twitted him because of a mark across his face, left by the rending claw of a great grizzly which he had slain in close fight.

The chief of his tribe possessed a beautiful daughter, whom all the young men desired in marriage. Scar-face also had fallen in love with her, but he felt ashamed to declare his passion because of his poverty. The maiden had already repulsed half the braves of his tribe. Why, he argued, should she accept him, poor and disfigured as he was?

One day he passed her as she sat outside her lodge. He cast a penetrating glance at her—a glance which was observed by one of her unsuccessful suitors, who sneeringly remarked:

"Scar-face would marry our chief's daughter! She does not desire a man without a blemish. Ha, Scar-face, now is your chance!"

Scar-face turned upon the jeerer, and in his quiet yet dignified manner remarked that it was his intention to ask the chief's daughter to be his wife. His announcement met with ridicule, but he took no notice of it and sought the girl.

He found her by the river, pulling rushes to make baskets. Approaching, he respectfully addressed her.

"I am poor," he said, "but my heart is rich in love for you. I have no wealth of furs or pemmican. I live by my bow and spear. I love you. Will you dwell with me in my lodge and be my wife?"

THE SUN-GOD'S DECREE

The girl regarded him with bright, shy eyes peering up through lashes as the morning sun peers through the branches.

"My husband would not be poor," she faltered, "for my father, the chief, is wealthy and has abundance in his lodge. But it has been laid upon me by the Sun-god that I may not marry."

---

[3] The reader cannot fail to discern the striking resemblance between this espisode and that of Una and the lion in Spenser's *Faerie Queene*.

"These are heavy words," said Scar-face sadly. "May they not be recalled?"

"On one condition only," replied the girl. "Seek the Sun-god and ask him to release me from my promise. If he consents to do so, request him to remove the scar from your face as a sign that I may know that he gives me to you."

Scar-face was sad at heart, for he could not believe that the Sun-god, having chosen such a beautiful maiden for himself, would renounce her. But he gave the chief's daughter his promise that he would seek out the god in his own bright country and ask him to grant his request.

For many moons Scar-face sought the home of the Sun-god. He traversed wide plains and dense forests, crossed rivers and lofty mountains, yet never a trace of the golden gates of the dwelling of the God of Light could he see.

Many inquiries did he make from the wild denizens of the forest—the wolf, the bear, the badger. But none was aware of the way to the home of the Sun-god. He asked the birds, but though they flew far they were likewise in ignorance of the road thither. At last he met a wolverine who told him that he had been there himself, and promised to set him on the way. For a long and weary season they marched onward, until at length they came to a great water, too broad and too deep to cross.

As Scar-face sat despondent on the bank bemoaning his case two beautiful swans advanced from the water, and, requesting him to sit on their backs, bore him across in safety. Landing him on the other side, they showed him which way to take and left him. He had not walked far when he saw a bow and arrows lying before him. But Scar-face was punctilious and would not pick them up because they did not belong to him. Not long afterward he encountered a beautiful youth of handsome form and smiling aspect.

"I have lost a bow and arrows," he said to Scar-face. "Have you seen them?"

Scar-face told him that he had seen them a little way back, and the handsome youth praised him for his honesty in not appropriating them. He further asked him where he was bound for.

"I am seeking the Sun in his home," replied the Indian, "and I believe that I am not far from my destination."

"You are right," replied the youth. "I am the son of the Sun, Apisirahts, the Morning Star, and I will lead you to the presence of my august father."

They walked onward for a little peace, and then Apisirahts pointed out a great lodge, glorious with golden light and decorated with an art more curious than any that Scar-face had ever beheld. At the entrance stood a beautiful woman, the mother of Morning Star, Kokomikis, the Moon-goddess, who welcomed the footsore Indian kindly and joyously.

THE CHASE OF THE SAVAGE BIRDS

Then the great Sun-god appeared, wondrous in his strength and beauty as the mighty planet over which he ruled. He too greeted Scar-face kindly, and requested him to be his guest and to hunt with his son. Scar-face and the youth gladly set out for the chase. But on departing the Sun-god warned them not to venture near the Great Water, as there dwelt savage birds which might slay Morning Star.

Scar-face tarried with the Sun, his wife, and child, fearful of asking his boon too speedily, and desiring to make as sure as possible of its being granted.

One day he and Morning Star hunted as usual, and the youth stole away, for he wished to slay the savage birds of which his father had spoken. But Scar-face followed, rescued the lad in imminent peril, and killed the monsters. The Sun was grateful to him for having saved his son from a terrible death, and asked him for what reason he had sought his lodge. Scar-face acquainted him with the circumstances of his love for the chief's daughter and of his quest. At once the Sun-god granted his desire.

"Return to the woman you love so much," he said, "return and make her yours. And as a sign that it is my will that she should be your wife, I make you whole."

With a motion of his bright hand the deity removed the unsightly scar. On quitting the Sun-country the god, his wife, and son presented Scar-face with many good gifts, and showed him a short route by which to return to Earth-land once more.

Scar-face soon reached home. When he sought his chief's daughter she did not know him at first, so rich was the gleaming attire he had obtained in the Sun-country. But when she at last recognized him she fell upon his breast with a glad cry. That same day she was made his wife. The happy pair raised a "medicine" lodge to the Sun-god, and henceforth Scar-face was called Smooth-face.

THE LEGEND OF POÏA

A variant of this beautiful story is as follows:

One summer morning a beautiful girl called Feather-woman, who had been sleeping outside her lodge among the long prairie grass, awoke just as the Morning Star was rising above the horizon. She gazed intently at it, and so beautiful did it seem that she fell deeply in love with it. She awakened her sister, who was lying beside her, and declared to her that she would marry nobody but the Morning Star. The people of her tribe ridiculed her because of what they considered her absurd preference; so she avoided them as much as possible, and wandered alone, eating her heart out in secret for love of the Morning Star, who seemed to her unapproachable.

One day she went alone to the river for water, and as she returned she beheld a young man standing before her. At first she took him for one of the young men of the tribe, and would have avoided him, but he said:

"I am the Morning Star. I beheld you gazing upward at me, and knew that you loved me. I returned your love, and have descended to ask you to go with me to my dwelling in the sky."

Feather-woman trembled violently, for she knew that he who spoke to her was a god, and replied hesitatingly that she must bid farewell to her father and mother. But this Morning Star would not permit. He took a rich yellow plume from his hair and directed her to hold this in one hand, while she held a juniper branch in the other. Then he commanded her to close her eyes, and when she opened them again she was in the Sky-country, standing before a great and shining lodge. Morning Star told her that this was the home of his parents, the Sun and Moon, and requested her to enter. It was daytime, so that the Sun was away on his diurnal round, but the Moon was at home. She welcomed Feather-woman as the wife of her son, as did the Sun himself when he returned. The Moon clothed her in a soft robe of buckskin, trimmed with elks' teeth. Feather-woman was very happy, and dwelt contentedly in the lodge of Morning Star. They had a little son, whom they called Star-boy. The Moon gave Feather-woman a root-digger, and told her that she could dig up all kinds of roots, but warned her on no account to dig up the large turnip which grew near the home of the Spider Man, telling her that it would bring unhappiness to all of them if she did so.

THE GREAT TURNIP

Feather-woman often saw the large turnip, but always avoided touching it. One day, however, her curiosity got the better of her, and she was tempted to see what might be underneath it. She laid her little son on the ground and dug until her root-digger stuck fast. Two large cranes came flying overhead. She begged these to help her. They did so, and sang a magic song which enabled them to uproot the turnip.

Now, although she was unaware of it, this very turnip filled up the hole through which Morning Star had brought her into the Sky-country. Gazing downward, she saw the camp of the Blackfeet where she had lived.

The smoke was ascending from the lodges, she could hear the song of the women as they went about their work. The sight made her homesick and lonely, and as she went back to her lodge she cried softly to herself. When she arrived Morning Star gazed earnestly at her, and said with a sorrowful expression of countenance: "You have dug up the sacred turnip."

The Moon and Sun were also troubled, and asked her the meaning of her sadness, and when she had told them they said that as she had disobeyed their injunction she must return to earth. Morning Star took her to the Spider Man, who let her down to earth by a web, and the people beheld her coming to earth like a falling star.

THE RETURN TO EARTH

She was welcomed by her parents, and returned with her child, whom she had brought with her from the Sky-country, to the home of her youth. But happiness never came back to her. She mourned ceaselessly for her husband, and one morning, climbing to the summit of a high mound, she watched the beautiful Morning Star rise above the horizon, just as on the day when she had first loved him. Stretching out her arms to the eastern sky, she besought him passionately to take her back. At length he spoke to her.

"It is because of your own sin," he said, "that you are forever shut out from the Sky-country. Your disobedience has brought sorrow upon yourself and upon all your people."

Her pleadings were in vain, and in despair she returned to her lodge, where her unhappy life soon came to a close. Her little son, Star-boy, was now an orphan, and the death of his grandparents deprived him of all his earthly kindred. He was a shy, retiring, timid boy, living in the deepest poverty, notwithstanding his exalted station as grandchild of the Sun. But the most noticeable thing about him was a scar which disfigured his face, because of which he was given the name of Poïa (Scar-face) by the wits of the tribe. As he grew older the scar became more pronounced, and ridicule and abuse were heaped upon him. When he became a man he fell in love with a maiden of surpassing beauty, the daughter of a great chief of his tribe. She, however, laughed him to scorn, and told him that she would marry him when he removed the scar from his face. Poïa, greatly saddened by her unkindness, consulted an old medicine-woman, to see whether the scar might not be removed. She could only tell him that the mark had been placed on his face by the Sun, and that the Sun alone could remove it. This was melancholy news for Poïa. How could he reach the abode of the Sun? Nevertheless, encouraged by the old woman, he resolved to make the attempt. Gratefully accepting her parting gift of pemmican and moccasins, he set off on a journey that was to last for many days.

THE BIG WATER

After climbing mountains and traversing forests and wandering over trackless prairies he arrived at the Big Water (that is to say, the Pacific Ocean), on the shores of which he sat down, praying and fasting for three days. On the third day, when the Sun was sinking behind the rim of the ocean, he saw a bright pathway leading straight to the abode of the Sun. He resolved to follow the shining trail, though he knew not what might lie before him in the great Sky-country. He arrived quite safely, however, at the wonderful lodge of the Sun. All night he hid himself outside the lodge, and in the morning the Sun, who was about to begin his daily journey, saw a ragged wayfarer lying by his door. He did not know that the intruder was his grandson, but, seeing that he had come from the Earth-country, he determined to kill him, and said so to his wife, the Moon. But she begged that the stranger's life should be spared, and Morning Star, who at that moment issued from the lodge, also gave Poïa his protection. Poïa lived very happily in the lodge of the Sun, and having on one occasion killed seven birds who were about to destroy Morning Star, he earned the gratitude of his grandparents. At the request of Morning Star the sun removed the scar on Poïa's face, and bade him return with a message to the Blackfeet. If they would honour him once a year in a Sun Dance he would consent to heal their sick. The secrets of the Sun Dance were taught to Poïa, two raven's feathers were placed in his hair, and he was given a robe of elk-skin. The latter, he was told, must only be worn by a virtuous woman, who should then dance the Sun Dance, so that the sick might be restored to health. From his father Poïa received an enchanted flute and a magic song, which would win the heart of the maid he loved.

Poïa came to earth by the Milky Way, or, as the Indians call it, the Wolf-trail, and communicated to the Blackfeet all that he had learned in the Sky-country. When they were thoroughly conversant with the Sun Dance he returned to the Sky-country, the home of his father, accompanied by his beautiful bride. Here they dwelt together happily, and Poïa and the Morning Star travelled together through the sky.

A BLACKFOOT DAY-AND-NIGHT MYTH

Many stories are told by the Blackfoot Indians of their creator, Nápi, and these chiefly relate to the manner in which he made the world and its inhabitants.

One myth connected with this deity tells how a poor Indian who had a wife and two children lived in the greatest indigence on roots and berries. This man had a dream in which he heard a voice command him to procure a large spider-web, which he was to hang on the trail of the animals where they passed through the forest, by which means he would obtain plenty of food. This he did, and on returning to the place in which he had hung the web he found deer and rabbits entangled in its magical meshes. These he killed for food, for which he was now never at a loss.

Returning with his game on his shoulders one morning, he discovered his wife perfuming herself with sweet pine, which she burned over the fire. He suspected that she was thus making herself attractive for the benefit of someone else, but, preserving silence, he told her that on the following day he would set his spider-web at a greater distance, as the game in the neighbouring forest was beginning to know the trap too well. Accordingly he went farther afield, and caught a deer, which he cut up, carrying part of its meat back with him to his lodge. He told his wife where the remainder of the carcass was to be found, and asked her to go and fetch it.

His wife, however, was not without her own suspicions, and, concluding that she was being watched by her husband, she halted at the top of the nearest hill and looked back to see if he was following her. But he was sitting where she had left him, so she proceeded on her way. When she was quite out of sight the Indian himself climbed the hill, and, seeing that she was not in the vicinity, returned to the camp. He inquired of his children where their mother went to gather firewood, and they pointed to a large patch of dead timber. Proceeding to the clump of leafless trees, the man instituted a thorough search, and after a while discovered a den of rattlesnakes. Now it was one of these reptiles with which his wife was in love, so the Indian in his wrath gathered fragments of dry wood and set the whole plantation in a blaze. Then he returned to his lodge and told his children what he had done, at the same time warning them that their mother would be very wrathful, and would probably attempt to kill them all. He further said that he would wait for her return, but that they had better run away, and that he would provide them with three things which they would find of use. He then handed to the children a stick, a stone, and a bunch of moss, which they were to throw behind them should their mother pursue them. The children at once ran away, and their father hung the spider-web over the door of the lodge. Meanwhile the woman had seen the blaze made by the dry timber-patch from a considerable distance, and in great anger turned and ran back to the lodge. Attempting to enter it, she was at once entangled in the meshes of the spider-web.

THE PURSUING HEAD

She struggled violently, however, and succeeded in getting her head through the opening, whereupon her husband severed it from her shoulders with his stone axe. He then ran out of the lodge and down the valley, hotly pursued by the woman's body, while her head rolled along the ground in chase of the children. The latter soon descried the grisly object rolling along in their tracks at a great speed, and one of them quickly threw the stick behind him as he had been told to do. Instantly a dense forest sprang up in their rear, which for a space retarded their horrible pursuer. The children made considerable headway, but once more the severed head made its appearance, gnashing its teeth in a frenzy of rage and rolling its eyes horribly, while it shrieked out threats which caused the children's blood to turn to water.

Then another of the boys threw the stone which he had been given behind him, and instantly a great mountain sprang up which occupied the land from sea to sea, so that the progress of the head was quite barred. It could perceive no means of overcoming this immense barrier, until it encountered two rams feeding, which it asked to make a way for it through the mountain, telling them that if they would do so it would marry the chief of the sheep. The rams made a valiant effort to meet this request, and again and again fiercely rushed at the mountain, till their horns were split and broken and they could butt no longer. The head, growing impatient, called upon a colony of ants which dwelt in the neighbourhood to tunnel a passage through the obstacle, and offered, if they were successful, to marry the chief ant as a recompense for their labours. The insects at once took up the task, and toiled incessantly until they had made a tunnel through which the head could roll.

THE FATE OF THE HEAD

The children were still running, but felt that the head had not abandoned pursuit. At last, after a long interval, they observed it rolling after them, evidently as fresh as ever. The child who had the bunch of moss now wet it and wrung out the water over their trail, and immediately an immense strait separated them from the land where they had been but a moment before. The head, unable to stop, fell into this great water and was drowned.

The children, seeing that their danger was past, made a raft and sailed back to the land from which they had come. Arrived there, they journeyed eastward through many countries, peopled by many different tribes of Indians, in order to reach their own territory. When they arrived there they found it occupied by tribes unknown to them, so they resolved to separate, one going north and the other south. One of them was shrewd and clever, and the other simple and ingenious. The shrewd boy is he who made the white people and instructed them in their arts. The other, the simple boy, made the Blackfeet, but, being very stupid, was unable to teach them anything. He it was who was called

Nápi. As for the mother's body, it continued to chase her husband, and is still following him, for she is the Moon and he is the Sun. If she succeeds in catching him she will slay him, and night will reign forevermore, but as long as he is able to evade her day and night will continue to follow one another.

NÁPI AND THE BUFFALO-STEALER

There was once a great famine among the Blackfeet. For months no buffaloes were killed, and the weaker members of the tribe dropped off one by one, while even the strong braves and hunters began to sink under the privation. The chief in despair prayed that the creator, Nápi, would send them food. Nápi, meanwhile, was far away in the south, painting the plumage of the birds in gorgeous tints. Nevertheless he heard the voice of the chief over all the distance, and hastened northward.

"Who has summoned me?" he demanded.

"It was I," said the chief humbly. "My people are starving, and unless relief comes soon I fear we must all perish."

"You shall have food," answered Nápi. "I will provide game for you."

Taking with him the chief's son, Nápi travelled toward the west. As they went the youth prayed earnestly to the Sun, the Moon, and the Morning Star, but his companion rebuked his impatience and bade him hold his peace. They crossed the Sweet Grass Hills, which Nápi had made from huge handfuls of herbage, and where he loved to rest. Still there was no sign of game. At length they reached a little lodge by the side of a river, and Nápi called a halt.

"There dwells the cause of your misfortunes," said he. "He who lives in that lodge is the Buffalo-stealer. He it is who has taken all the herds from the prairies, so that there is none left."

To further his design, Nápi took the shape of a dog, and turned the youth into a stick. Not long afterward the little son of Buffalo-stealer was passing that way, and immediately desired to take the little dog home with him.

"Very well," said his mother; "take that stick and drive it to the lodge."

But the boy's father frowned angrily.

"I do not like the look of the beast," he said. "Send it away."

The boy refused to part with the dog, and his mother wanted the stick to gather roots with, so the father was obliged to give way. Still he did not show any goodwill to the dog. The following day he went out of the lodge, and in a short time returned with a buffalo, which he skinned and prepared for cooking. His wife, who was in the woods gathering berries, came home toward evening, and at her husband's bidding cooked part of the buffalo-meat. The little boy incurred his father's anger again by giving a piece of meat to the dog.

"Have I not told you," cried Buffalo-stealer irately, "that he is an evil thing? Do not touch him."

That night when all was silent Nápi and the chief's son resumed their human form and supped off the buffalo-meat.

"It is Buffalo-stealer who keeps the herds from coming near the Blackfoot camp," said Nápi. "Wait till morning and see."

THE HERDS OF BUFFALO-STEALER

In the morning they were once more dog and stick. When the woman and her child awoke they set off for the woods again, the former taking the stick to dig for roots, the latter calling for his little dog to accompany him. Alas! When they reached the spot they had fixed upon for root-gathering operations both dog and stick had vanished! And this was the reason for their disappearance. As the dog was trotting through the wood he had observed an opening like the mouth of a cavern, all but concealed by the thick undergrowth, and in the aperture he perceived a buffalo. His short, sharp barking attracted the attention of the stick, which promptly wriggled snake-wise after him. Within the cavern were great herds of deer and buffalo, enough to provide the Blackfeet with food for years and years. Nápi ran among them, barking, and they were driven out to the prairie.

When Buffalo-stealer returned and discovered his loss his wrath knew no bounds. He questioned his wife and son, but they denied all knowledge of the affair.

"Then," said he, "it is that wretched little dog of yours. Where is he now?"

But the child could not tell him.

"We lost him in the woods," said he.

"I shall kill him," shouted the man, "and I shall break the stick as well!"

Nápi overheard the threat, and clung to the long hair of an old buffalo. He advised the stick to conceal itself in the buffalo's hair also, and so the twain escaped unnoticed from the cave, much as did Ulysses from the Cyclops' cavern. Once again they took the form of men, and drove a herd of buffalo to the Blackfoot camp, while Buffalo-stealer and his family sought them in vain.

The people met them with delighted acclamations, and the famine was at an end. Yet there were still some difficulties in the way, for when they tried to get the herd into the enclosure a large grey bird so frightened the animals with its dismal note that they refused to enter. This occurred so often that Nápi suspected that the grey bird was no other than Buffalo-stealer. Changing himself into an otter, he lay by the side of a river and pretended to be dead. The greedy bird saw what he thought to be a dead otter, and pounced upon it, whereupon Nápi seized him by the leg and bore him off to the camp. By way of punishment he was tied over the smoke-hole of the wigwam, where his grey feathers soon became black and his life a burden to him.

"Spare me!" he cried. "Let me return to my wife and child. They will surely starve."

His piteous appeals moved the heart of Nápi, and he let him go, but not without an admonition.

"Go," said he, "and hunt for food, that you may support your wife and child. But do not take more than you need, or you shall die."

The bird did as he was bidden. But to this day the feathers of the raven are black, and not grey.

THE STORY OF KUTOYIS

There once lived on the banks of the Missouri an old couple who had one daughter, their only child. When she grew to be a woman she had a suitor who was cruel and overbearing, but as she loved him her parents offered no opposition to their marriage. Indeed, they gave the bride the best part of their possessions for a dowry, so that she and her husband were rich, while her father and mother lived in a poor lodge and had very little to eat. The wicked son-in-law took advantage of their kindness in every way. He forced the old man to accompany him on his hunting expeditions, and then refused to share the game with him. Sometimes one would kill a buffalo and sometimes the other, but always it was the younger man who got the best of the meat and who made himself robes and moccasins from the hide.

Thus the aged couple were nearly perishing from cold and hunger. Only when her husband was out hunting would the daughter venture to carry a morsel of meat to her parents.

On one occasion the younger man called in his overbearing way to his father-in-law, bidding him help in a buffalo-hunt. The old man, reduced by want almost to a skeleton, was too much afraid of the tyrant to venture to disobey him, so he accompanied him in the chase. Ere long they encountered a fine buffalo, whereupon both drew their bows and fired. But it was the arrow of the elder man which pierced the animal and brought it to the ground. The old man set himself to skin the buffalo, for his son-in-law never shared in these tasks, but left them to his companion. While he was thus engaged the latter observed a drop of blood on one of his arrows which had fallen to the ground.

Thinking that even a drop of blood was better than nothing, he replaced the arrow in its quiver and set off home. As it happened, no more of the buffalo than that fell to his share, the rest being appropriated by his son-in-law.

On his return the old man called to his wife to heap fuel on the fire and put on the kettle. She, thinking he had brought home some buffalo-meat, hastened to do his bidding. She waited curiously till the water in the kettle had boiled; then to her surprise she saw him place in it an arrow with a drop of blood on it.

HOW KUTOYIS WAS BORN

"Why do you do that?" she asked.

"Something will come of it," he replied. "My spirit tells me so."

They waited in silence.

Then a strange sound was heard in their lonely little lodge—the crying of a child. Half fearfully, half curiously, the old couple lifted the lid of the kettle, and there within was a little baby boy.

"He shall bring us good luck," said the old Indian.

They called the child Kutoyis—that is, "Drop of Blood"—and wrapped him up as is customary with Indian babies.

"Let us tell our son-in-law," said the old man, "that it is a little girl, and he will let it live. If we say it is a boy he will surely kill it."

Kutoyis became a great favourite in the little lodge to which he had come. He was always laughing, and his merriment won the hearts of the old people. One day, while they thought him much too young to speak, they were astonished to hear his voice.

"Lash me up and hang me from the lodge pole," said he, "and I shall become a man."

When they had recovered from their astonishment they lashed him to the lodge pole. In a moment he had burst the lashings and grown before their eyes into a tall, strong man. Looking round the lodge, which seemed scarcely large enough to hold him, Kutoyis perceived that there was no food about.

"Give me some arrows," said he, "and I will bring you food."

"We have no arrows," replied the old man, "only four arrowheads."

Kutoyis fetched some wood, from which he cut a fine bow, and shafts to fit the flint arrowheads. He begged the old Indian to lead him to a good hunting-ground, and when he had done so they quickly killed a magnificent buffalo.

Meanwhile the old Indian had told Kutoyis how badly his son-in-law had treated him, and as they were skinning the buffalo who should pass by but the subject of their conversation. Kutoyis hid behind the dead animal to see what would happen, and a moment later the angry voice of the son-in-law was heard.

Getting no reply, the cowardly hunter fitted an arrow to his bow and shot it at his father-in-law. Enraged at the cruel act, Kutoyis rose from his hiding-place behind the dead buffalo and fired all his arrows at the young man, whom he slew. He afterward gave food in plenty to the old man and his wife, and bade them return to their home. They were delighted to find themselves once more free from persecution, but their daughter wept so much that finally Kutoyis asked her whether she would have another husband or whether she wished to follow her first spouse to the Land of Shadows, as she must do if she persisted in lamenting him.

The lady chose the former alternative as the lesser evil, and Kutoyis found her an excellent husband, with whom she lived happily for a long time.

KUTOYIS ON HIS TRAVELS

At length Kutoyis tired of his monotonous life, and desired to see more of the world. So his host directed him to a distant village, where he was welcomed by two old women. They set before their handsome guest the best fare at their disposal, which was buffalo-meat of a rather unattractive appearance.

"Is there no good meat?" queried Kutoyis.

The old women explained that one of the lodges was occupied by a fierce bear, who seized upon all the good meat and left only the dry, poor sort for his neighbours. Without hesitation Kutoyis went out and killed a buffalo calf, which he presented to the women, desiring them to place the best parts of the meat in a prominent position outside the lodge, where the big bear could not fail to see it.

This they did, and sure enough one of the bear-cubs shortly passed by and seized the meat. Kutoyis, who had been lying in wait, rushed out and hit the animal as hard as he could. The cub carried his tale of woe to his father, and the big bear, growling threats of vengeance, gathered his whole family round him and rushed to the lodge of the old women, intending to kill the bold hunter.

However, Kutoyis was more than a match for all of them, and very soon the bears were slain. Still he was unsatisfied, and longed for further adventures.

"Tell me," said he, "where shall I find another village?"

THE WRESTLING WOMAN

"There is a village by the Big River," said the old women, "but you must not go there, for a wicked woman dwells in it who wrestles with and slays all who approach."

No sooner did Kutoyis hear this than he determined to seek the village, for his mission was to destroy evil beings who were a danger to his fellow-men. So in spite of the dissuasions of the old women he departed.

As he had been warned, the woman came out of her lodge on the approach of the stranger and invited him to wrestle with her.

"I cannot," said he, pretending to be frightened.

The woman mocked and jeered at him, while he made various excuses, but all the time he was observing how the land lay. When he drew nearer he saw that she had covered the ground with sharp flints, over which she had strewn grass. At last he said: "Very well, I will wrestle with you."

It was no wonder that she had killed many braves, for she was very strong. But Kutoyis was still stronger. With all her skill she could not throw him, and at last she grew tired, and was herself thrown on the sharp flints, on which she bled to death. The people rejoiced greatly when they heard of her death, and Kutoyis was universally acclaimed as a hero.

Kutoyis did many other high deeds before he departed to the Shadowland, and when he went he left sorrow in many lodges.

II

IROQUOIS MYTHS AND LEGENDS

IROQUOIS GODS AND HEROES

THE MYTHS of the Iroquois are of exceptional interest because of the portraits they present of several semi-historical heroes. The earliest substratum of the myths of this people deals with the adventures of their principal deity, Hi'nun, the Thunder-god, who, with his brother, the West Wind, finally overcame and exterminated the powerful race of Stone Giants. Coming to a later period, we find that a number of legends cluster round the names of the chiefs Atotarho and Hiawatha, who in all probability at one time really existed. These present a good instance of the rapidity with which myth gathers round a famous name. Atotarho, the mighty warrior, is now regarded as the wizard *par excellence* of the Iroquois, but probably this does not result from the fact that he was cunning and cruel, as some writers on the tribe appear to think, but from the circumstance that as a great warrior he was clothed in a garment of serpents, and these reptiles, besides being looked upon as powerful war-physic, also possessed a deep magical significance. The original Hiawatha (He who seeks the Wampum-belt) is pictured as the father of a long line of persons of the same name, who appear to have been important functionaries in the tribal government. To him was ascribed the honour of having established the great confederacy of the Iroquois, which so long rendered them formidable opponents to the tribes which surrounded them. Like many other heroes in myth—the Celtic Mananan, for example—Hiawatha possessed a magic canoe which would obey his slightest behest, and in which he finally quitted the terrestrial sphere for that shadowy region to which all heroes finally take their departure.

HI'NUN

Many interesting myths are related of the manner in which Hi'nun destroyed the monsters and giants which infested the early world. A hunter, caught in a heavy thunder-shower, took refuge in the woods.

Crouching under the shelter of a great tree, he became aware of a mysterious voice which urged him to follow it. He was conscious of a sensation of slowly rising from the earth, and he soon found himself gazing downward from a point near the clouds, the height of many trees from the ground. He was surrounded by beings who had all the appearance of men, with one among them who seemed to be their chief. They asked him to cast his eyes toward the earth and tell them whether he could see a huge water-serpent. Unable to descry such a monster, the chief anointed his eyes with a sacred ointment, which gave him supernatural sight and permitted him to behold a dragon-like shape in the watery depths far below him. The chief commanded one of his warriors to dispatch the monster, but arrow after arrow failed to transfix it, whereupon the hunter was requested to display his skill as an archer. Drawing his bow, he took careful aim. The arrow whizzed down the depths and was speedily lost to sight, but a terrible commotion arose in the lake below, the body of the great serpent leaping from the blood-stained water with dreadful writhings and contortions. So appalling was the din that rose up to them that even the heavenly beings by whom the hunter was surrounded fell into a great trembling; but gradually the tempest of sound subsided, and the huge bulk of the mortally wounded serpent sank back into the lake, the surface of which became gradually more still, until finally all was peace once more. The chief thanked the hunter for the service he had rendered, and he was conducted back to earth. Thus was man first brought into contact with the beneficent Hi'nun, and thus did he learn the existence of a power which would protect him from forces unfriendly to humanity.

THE THUNDERERS

Once in early Iroquois days three braves set out upon an expedition. After they had journeyed for some time a misfortune occurred, one of their number breaking his leg. The others fashioned a litter with the object of carrying him back to his home, as Indian custom exacted. Retracing their steps, they came to a range of high mountains, the steep slopes of which taxed their strength to the utmost. To rest themselves they placed the disabled man on the ground and withdrew to a little distance.

"Why should we be thus burdened with a wounded man?" said one to the other.

"You speak truly," was the rejoinder. "Why should we, indeed, since his hurt has come upon him by reason of his own carelessness?"

As they spoke their eyes met in a meaning glance, and one of them pointed to a deep hole or pit opening in the side of the mountain at a little distance from the place where they were sitting. Returning to the injured man, they raised him as if about to proceed on the journey, and when passing the brink of the pit suddenly hurled him into it with great force. Then without loss of time they set their faces homeward. When they arrived in camp they reported that their comrade had died of wounds received in fight, but that he had not fallen into the enemy's hands, having received careful attention from them in his dying moments and honourable burial. The unfortunate man's aged mother was prostrate with grief at the sad news, but was somewhat relieved to think that her son had been kindly ministered to at the end.

When the brave who had been thrown into the pit regained his senses after the severe fall he had sustained he perceived a man of venerable aspect bending over him solicitously. When this person saw that the young man had regained consciousness he asked him what had been the intention of his comrades in so cruelly casting him into that abyss. The young man replied that his fellows had become tired of carrying him and had thus rid themselves of him. The old hermit—for so he seemed to be—made a hasty examination of the Indian's injuries, and announced that he would speedily cure him, on one condition. The other pledged his word to accept this, whatever it might be, whereupon the recluse told him that all he required was that he should hunt for him and bring home to him such game as he should slay. To this the brave gave a ready assent. The old man lost no time in performing his part of the bargain. He applied herbs to his injuries and assiduously tended his guest, who made a speedy and satisfactory recovery. The grateful warrior, once more enabled to follow the chase, brought home many trophies of his skill as a hunter to the cave on the mountainside, and soon the pair had formed a strong attachment. One day, when in the forest, the warrior encountered an enormous bear, which he succeeded in slaying after a desperate struggle. As he was pondering how best he could remove it to the cave he became aware of a murmur of voices behind him, and glancing round he saw three men, or beings in the shape of men, clad in strange diaphanous garments, standing near. In reply to his question as to what brought them there, they told him that they were the Thunderers, or people of Hi'nun, whose mission it was to keep the earth in good order for the benefit of humanity, and to slay or destroy every agency inimical to mankind. They told him that the old man with whom he had been residing was by no means the sort of person he seemed to think, and that they had come to earth with the express intention of compassing his destruction. In this they requested his assistance, and promised him that if he would vouchsafe it he would speedily be transported back to his mother's lodge. Overjoyed at this proposal, the hunter did not scruple to return to the cave and tell the hermit that he had killed the bear, which he wished his help in bringing home. The old man seemed very uneasy, and begged him to examine the sky and tell him whether he perceived the least sign of clouds. The young brave reassured him and told him that not a cloud was to be seen, whereupon, emerging from his shelter, he made for the spot where the bear was lying. Hastily picking up the carcass, he requested his companion to place it all on his shoulders, which the young man did, expressing surprise at his great strength. He had proceeded with his burden for some distance when a terrific clap of thunder burst from the menacing black clouds which had speedily gathered overhead. In great terror the old man threw down his load and commenced to run with an agility which belied his years, but when a second peal broke forth he suddenly assumed the shape of a gigantic porcupine, which dashed through the undergrowth, discharging its quills like arrows as it ran. A veritable hail of thunderbolts now crashed down upon the creature's spiny back. As it reached the entrance to the cave one larger than the rest struck it with such tremendous force that it rolled dead into its den.

Then the Thunderers swooped down from the sky in triumph, mightily pleased at the death of their victim. The young hunter now requested them to discharge the promise they had made him to transport him back to his mother's lodge; so, having fastened cloud-wings on his shoulders, they speedily brought him thither, carrying him carefully through the air and depositing him just outside the hut. The widow was delighted to see her son, whom she had believed to be long dead, and the Thunderers were so pleased with the assistance he had lent them that they asked him to accompany them in their monster-destroying mission every spring. He assented, and on one of these expeditions flew earthward to drink from a certain pool. When he rejoined his companions they observed that the water with which his lips were moist had caused them to shine as if smeared with oil. At their request he indicated the pool from which he had drunk, and they informed him that in its depths there dwelt a monster for which they had searched for years. With that they hurled a great thunderbolt into the pool, which immediately dried up, revealing an immense grub of the species which destroys the standing crops. The monster was, indeed, the King of Grubs, and his death set back the conspiracies of his kind for many generations. The youth subsequently returned to earth, and having narrated to the members of his tribe the services which Hi'nun had performed on their behalf, they considered it fitting to institute a special worship of the deity, and, in fact, to make him supreme god of their nation. Even today many Iroquois allude to Hi'nun as their grandfather, and evince extraordinary veneration at the mention of his name.

HIAWATHA

Much confusion exists with regard to the true status of the reputed Iroquois hero Hiawatha. We find him variously represented as a historical personage and a mythical demigod, and as belonging to both the

Iroquois and the Algonquins. In solid history and in the wildest myth he is a figure of equal importance. This confusion is largely due to the popularity of Longfellow's poem *Hiawatha,* which by its very excellence has given the greatest prominence to the fallacies it contains. The fact is that Longfellow, following in the path of Schoolcraft, has really confused *two* personages in the character of Hiawatha, one the entirely mythical Manabozho, or Michabo—which name he at first intended to bestow on his poem—and the other the almost wholly historical Hiawatha. Manabozho, according to tradition, was a demigod of the Ojibways, and to him, and not to Hiawatha, must be credited the exploits described in the poem. There is no doubt that myths have grown up round the name of the Iroquois hero, for myth is the ivy that binds all historical ruins and makes them picturesque to the eye; but it has been proved that there is a solid structure of fact behind the legendary stories of Hiawatha, and even the period of his activity has been fixed with tolerable accuracy by modern American historians.

Hiawatha, or Hai-en-Wat-ha, was a chief of Iroquois stock, belonging either to the Onondaga or the Mohawk tribe. His most important feat was the union of the Five Nations of the Iroquois into a Grand League, an event which was of more than national significance, since it so largely affected the fortunes of European peoples when they afterward fought for American supremacy. As the Five Nations are known to have come together in the sixteenth century, it follows that Hiawatha must have lived and worked about that time. In later days the League was called the Six Nations, and still more recently the Seven Nations.

When the Iroquois, or "Long House People," were found by the French and Dutch they occupied the western part of what is now New York State, and were at a much more advanced stage of culture than most of the Indian tribes. They tilled the ground, cultivating maize and tobacco, and were skilled in the arts of war and diplomacy. They were greatly strengthened by the Grand League, or "Kayanerenh Kowa," which, as has been said, was founded by the chief Hiawatha, and were the most important of the North American tribes.

If we look to tradition for an account of the origin of the Grand League, we learn that the union was effected by Hiawatha in the fourteenth century. The Hurons and Iroquois, we are told, were at one time one people, but later they separated, the Hurons going to the lake which is named after them, and the Iroquois to New York, where their five tribes were united under a General Council. But tradition is quite evidently wrong in assigning so early a date to this important event, for one of the two branches of the Iroquois family (that which comprises the Mohawks and the Oneidas) has left but few traces of an early occupation, and these, in the shape of some old town-sites, are judged to belong to the latter part of the sixteenth century.

The early connexion between the Iroquois and the Hurons, and their subsequent separation, remains undisputed. The Iroquois family was divided into two branches, the Sinnekes (Onondaga, Cayugas, and Senecas) and the Caniengas (Mohawks and Oneidas), of which the sub-divisions composed the Five Nations. The Sinnekes had established themselves in the western portion of New York, and the Caniengas at Hochelaga (Montreal) and elsewhere on the St. Lawrence, where they lived amicably enough with their Algonquin neighbours. But in 1560 a quarrel arose between the Caniengas and the Algonquins, in which the latter called in the aid of the Hurons. This was the beginning of a long war, in which the Caniengas had the worst of it. Gradually the Caniengas were driven along the shores of Lake Champlain and Lake George till they reached the valley of the Mohawk River, where they established themselves in a country bordering on that of the Onondagas.

Now the Onondagas were a formidable tribe, fierce and warlike, and the Caniengas, being long accustomed to war, were not the most peaceable of nations, and ere long there was trouble between them, while both were at war with the Hurons. At the head of the Onondagas was the great chief Atotarho, whose sanguinary exploits and crafty stratagems had become the dread of the neighbouring peoples, and among his warriors was the generous Hiawatha. Hiawatha was filled with horror at the sight of the suffering caused by Atotarho's expeditions, and already his stateman's mind was forming projects of peace. He saw that in confederation lay the means not only of preserving peace among his people, but of withstanding alien foes as well. In two consecutive years he called an assembly to consider his plan, but on each occasion the grim presence of Atotarho made discussion impossible. Hiawatha in despair fled from the land of the Onondaga, journeyed eastward through the country of the Oneidas, and at last took up his residence among the Mohawks, into which tribe he was adopted. It has been said by some authorities, and the idea does not lack probability, that Hiawatha was originally a Mohawk, and that he spent some time among the Onondagas, afterward returning to his own people. At all events, the Mohawks proved more amenable to reason than the Onondagas had done. Among the chiefs of his adopted tribe Hiawatha found one—Dekanewidah—who fell in with his confederation plans, and agreed to work along with him. Messengers were dispatched to the Oneidas, who bade them return in a year, at the end of which period negotiations were renewed. The result was that the Oneidas' chiefs signed a treaty inaugurating the Kayanerenh Kowa. An embassy to the Onondagas was fruitless, as Atotarho persistently obstructed the new scheme; but later, when the Kayanerenh Kowa embraced the Cayugas, messages were once more sent to the powerful Onondagas, diplomatically suggesting that Atotarho should take the lead in the Grand Council. The grim warrior was mollified by this sop to his vanity, and condescended to accept the proposal. Not only that, but he soon became an enthusiastic worker in the cause of confederation, and secured the inclusion of the Senecas in the League.

The confederacy of the Five Nations was now complete, and the "Silver Chain," as their Grand Council was called, met together on the shores of the Salt Lake. The number of chiefs chosen from each tribe bore some relation to its numerical status, the largest number, fourteen, being supplied by the Onondagas. The office of representative in the Council was to be a hereditary one, descending in the female line, as with the Picts of Scotland and other primitive peoples, and never from father to son.

So powerful did the League become that the name of "Long House People" was held in the greatest awe. They annihilated their ancient enemies, the Hurons, and they attacked and subdued the Micmacs, Mohicans, Pawnees, Algonquins, Cherokees, and many other tribes. The effect of the League on British history is incalculable. When the Frenchman Champlain arrived in 1611 he interfered on behalf of the Hurons, an action whose far-reaching consequences he could not foresee, but from that period dated the hatred of the Iroquois for the French which ensured Britain's success in the long struggle between the European nations in America. Without the assistance of the native factor, who shall say how the struggle might have ended?

But the Iroquois were not altogether a bloodthirsty people. A strong bond of brotherhood existed between the Five Nations, among themselves they were kind and gentle, and in part at least Hiawatha's dream of peace was realized. It is not, of course, very easy to say how far Hiawatha intended the scheme of universal brotherhood with which he is credited. Whether he conceived a Grand League embracing all the nations of the earth or whether his full ambition was realized in the union of the Five Nations is a point which history does not make clear. But even in the more limited sense his work was a great one, and the lofty and noble character which Longfellow has given to his hero seems not unsuited to the actual Hiawatha, who realizes the ideal of the "noble savage" more fully, perhaps, than anyone else in the annals of primitive peoples.

As in the case of King Arthur and Dietrich of Berne, many myths soon gathered round the popular and revered name of Hiawatha. Among barbarians three, or even two, generations usually suffice to render a great and outstanding figure mythical. But one prefers to think of this Iroquois statesman as a real man, a bright particular star in a dark sky of savagery and ignorance.

THE STONE GIANTS

The Iroquois believed that in early days there existed a malignant race of giants whose bodies were fashioned out of stone. It is difficult to say how the idea of such beings arose, but it is possible that the generally distributed conception of a gigantic race springing from Mother Earth was in this instance fused with another belief that stones and rocks composed the earth's bony framework. We find an example of this belief in the beautiful old Greek myth of Deucalion and Pyrrha, which much resembles that of Noah. When after the great flood which submerged Hellas the survivors' ship grounded upon Mount Parnassus they inquired of the oracle of Themis in what manner the human race might be restored. They were bidden by the oracle to veil themselves and to throw the bones of their mother behind them. These they interpreted to mean the stones of the earth. Picking up loose pieces of stone, they cast them over their shoulders, and from those thrown by Deucalion there sprang men, while those cast by Pyrrha became women.

These Stone Giants of the Iroquois, dwelling in the far west, took counsel with one another and resolved to invade the Indian territory and exterminate the race of men. A party of Indians just starting on the warpath were apprised of the invasion, and were bidden by the gods to challenge the giants to combat. This they did, and the opposing bands faced each other at a spot near a great gulf. But as the monsters advanced upon their human enemies the god of the west wind, who was lying in wait for them, swooped down upon the Titans, so that they were hurled over the edge of the gulf, far down into the dark abyss below, where they perished miserably.

THE PIGMIES

In contradistinction to their belief in giants, the Iroquois imagined the existence of a race of pigmies, who had many of the attributes of the Teutonic gnomes. They were responsible for the beauty of terrestrial scenery, which they carved and sculptured in cliff, scar, and rock, and, like the thunder-gods, they protected the human race against the many monsters which infested the world in early times.

WITCHES AND WITCHCRAFT

The Iroquois belief in witchcraft was very strong, and the following tale is supposed to account for the origin of witches and sorcery. A boy who was out hunting found a snake the colours of whose skin were so intensely beautiful that he resolved to capture it. He caught it and tended it carefully, feeding it on birds and small game, and housing it in a little bowl made of bark, which he filled with water. In the bottom of the bowl he placed down, small feathers, and wood fibre, and on going to feed the snake he discovered that these things had become living beings. From this he gathered that the reptile was endowed with supernatural powers, and he found that other articles placed in the water along with it soon showed signs of life. He procured more snakes and placed them in the bowl. Observing some men of the tribe rubbing ointment on their eyes to enable them to see more clearly, he used some of the water from the bowl in which the snakes were immersed upon his own, and lo! he found on climbing a tall tree that nothing was hidden from his sight, which pierced all intervening obstacles. He could see far into the earth, where lay hidden precious stones and rich minerals. His sight pierced the trunks of trees; he could see through mountains, and could discern objects lying deep down in the bed of a river.

He concluded that the greater the number of reptiles the snake-liquid contained the more potent would it become. Accordingly he captured several snakes, and suspended them over his bowl in such a manner that the essential oil they contained dropped into the water, with the result that the activity of the beings which had been so strangely bred in it was increased. In course of time he found that by merely placing one of his fingers in the liquid and pointing it at any person he could instantly bewitch him. He added some roots to the water in the bowl, some of which he then drank. By blowing this from his mouth a great light was produced, by rubbing his eyes with it he could see in the dark, and by other applications of it he could render himself invisible, or take the shape of a snake. If he dipped an arrow into the liquid and discharged it at any living being it would kill it although it might not strike it. Not content with discovering this magic fluid, the youth resolved to search for antidotes to it, and these he collected.

A "MEDICINE" LEGEND

A similar legend is told by the Senecas to account for the origin of their "medicine." Nearly two hundred years ago—in the savage estimation this is a very great period of time—an Indian went into the woods on a hunting expedition. One night while asleep in his solitary camp he was awakened by a great noise of singing and drum-beating, such as is heard at festivals. Starting up, he made his way to the place whence the sounds came, and although he could not see anyone there he observed a heap of corn and a large squash vine with three squashes on it, and three ears of corn which lay apart from the rest. Feeling very uneasy, he once more pursued his hunting operations, and when night came again laid himself down to rest. But his sleep was destined to be broken yet a second time, and awaking he perceived a man bending over him, who said in menacing tones:

"Beware: what you saw was sacred. You deserve to die."

A rustling among the branches denoted the presence of a number of people, who, after some hesitation, gathered round the hunter, and informed him that they would pardon his curiosity and would tell him their secret. "The great medicine for wounds," said the man who had first awakened him, "is squash and corn. Come with me and I will teach you how to make and apply it."

With these words he led the hunter to the spot at which he had surprised the "medicine"-making operations the previous night, where he beheld a great fire and a strange-looking laurel-bush, which seemed as if made of iron. Chanting a weird song, the people circled slowly round the bush to the accompaniment of a rattling of gourd-shells. On the hunter's asking them to explain this procedure, one of them heated a stick and thrust it right through his cheek. He immediately applied some of the "medicine" to the wound, so that it healed instantly. Having thus demonstrated the power of the drug, they sang a tune which they called the "medicine-song," which their pupil learnt by heart.

The hunter then turned to depart, and all at once he saw that the beings who surrounded him were not human, as he had thought, but animals—foxes, bears, and beavers—who fled as he looked at them. Surprised and even terrified at the turn matters had taken, he made his way homeward with all speed, conning over the prescription which the strange beings had given him the while. They had told him to take one stalk of corn, to dry the cob and pound it very fine, then to take one squash, cut it up and pound it, and to mix the whole with water from a running stream, near its source. This prescription he used with very great success among his people, and it proved the origin of the great "medicine" of the Senecas. Once a year at the season when the deer changes his coat they prepare it as the forest folk did, singing the weird song and dancing round it to the rhythmic accompaniment of the gourd-shell rattles, while they burn tobacco to the gods.

GREAT HEAD AND THE TEN BROTHERS

It was commonly believed among the Iroquois Indians that there existed a curious and malevolent being whom they called Great Head. This odd creature was merely an enormous head poised on slender legs. He made his dwelling on a rugged rock, and directly he saw any living person approach he would growl fiercely in true ogre fashion: "I see thee, I see thee! Thou shalt die."

Far away in a remote spot an orphaned family of ten boys lived with their uncle. The older brothers went out every day to hunt, but the younger ones, not yet fitted for so rigorous a life, remained at home with their uncle, or at least did not venture much beyond the immediate vicinity of their lodge. One day the hunters did not return at their usual hour. As the evening passed without bringing any sign of the missing youths the little band at home became alarmed. At length the eldest of the boys left in the lodge volunteered to go in search of his brothers. His uncle consented, and he set off, but he did not return.

In the morning another brother said: "I will go to seek my brothers." Having obtained permission, he went, but he also did not come back. Another and another took upon himself the task of finding the lost hunters, but of the searchers as well as of those sought for there was no news forthcoming. At length only the youngest of the lads remained at home, and to his entreaties to be allowed to seek his brothers the uncle turned a deaf ear, for he feared to lose the last of his young nephews.

One day when uncle and nephew were out in the forest the latter fancied he heard a deep groan, which seemed to proceed from the earth exactly under his feet. They stopped to listen. The sound was repeated—unmistakably a human groan. Hastily they began digging in the earth, and in a moment or two came upon a man covered with mould and apparently unconscious.

The pair carried the unfortunate one to their lodge, where they rubbed him with bear's oil till he recovered consciousness. When he was able to speak he could give no explanation of how he came to be buried alive. He had been out hunting, he said, when suddenly his mind became a blank, and he remembered nothing more till he found himself in the lodge with the old man and the boy. His hosts begged the stranger to stay with them, and they soon discovered that he was no ordinary mortal, but a powerful magician. At times he behaved very strangely. One night, while a great storm raged without, he tossed restlessly on his couch instead of going to sleep. At last he sought the old uncle.

"Do you hear that noise?" he said. "That is my brother, Great Head, who is riding on the wind. Do you not hear him howling?"

The old man considered this astounding speech for a moment; then he asked: "Would he come here if you sent for him?"

"No," said the other, thoughtfully, "but we might bring him here by magic. Should he come you must have food ready for him, in the shape of huge blocks of maple-wood, for that is what he lives on."

The stranger departed in search of his brother Great Head, taking with him his bow, and on the way he came across a hickory-tree, whose roots provided him with arrows. About midday he drew near to the dwelling of his brother, Great Head. In order to see without being seen, he changed himself into a mole, and crept through the grass till he saw Great Head perched on a rock, frowning fiercely. "I see thee!" he growled, with his wild eyes fixed on an owl. The man-mole drew his bow and shot an arrow at Great Head. The arrow became larger and larger as it flew toward the monster, but it returned to him who had fired it, and as it did so it regained its natural size. The man seized it and rushed back the way he had come. Very soon he heard Great Head in pursuit, puffing and snorting along on the wings of a hurricane. When the creature had almost overtaken him he turned and discharged another arrow. Again and again he repulsed his pursuer in this fashion, till he lured him to the lodge where his benefactors lived. When Great Head burst into the house the uncle and nephew began to hammer him vigorously with mallets. To their surprise the monster broke into laughter, for he had recognized his brother and was very pleased to see him. He ate the maple-blocks they brought him with a hearty appetite, whereupon they told him the story of the missing hunters.

"I know what has become of them," said Great Head. "They have fallen into the hands of a witch. If this young man," indicating the nephew, "will accompany me, I will show him her dwelling, and the bones of his brothers."

The youth, who loved adventure, and was besides very anxious to learn the fate of his brothers, at once consented to seek the home of the witch. So he and Great Head started off, and lost no time in getting to the place. They found the space in front of the lodge strewn with dry bones, and the witch sitting in the doorway singing. When she saw them she muttered the magic word which turned living people into dry bones, but on Great Head and his companion it had no effect whatsoever. Acting on a prearranged signal, Great Head and the youth attacked the witch and killed her. No sooner had she expired than her flesh turned into birds and beasts and fishes. What was left of her they burned to ashes.

Their next act was to select the bones of the nine brothers from among the heap, and this they found no easy task. But at last it was accomplished, and Great Head said to his companion: "I am going home to my rock. When I pass overhead in a great storm I will bid these bones arise, and they will get up and return with you."

The youth stood alone for a little while till he heard the sound of a fierce tempest. Out of the hurricane Great Head called to the brothers to arise. In a moment they were all on their feet, receiving the conggratulations of their younger brother and each other, and filled with joy at their reunion.

THE SENECA'S REVENGE

A striking story is told of a Seneca youth who for many years and through a wearisome captivity nourished the hope of vengeance so dear to the Indian soul. A certain tribe of the Senecas had settled on the shores of Lake Erie, when they were surprised by their ancient enemies the Illinois, and in spite of a stout resistance many of them were slain, and a woman and a boy taken prisoner. When the victors halted for the night they built a great fire and proceeded to celebrate their success by singing triumphant songs, in which they commanded the boy to join them. The lad pretended that he did not know their language, but said that he would sing their song in his own tongue, to which they assented; but instead of a pæan in their praise he sang a song of vengeance, in which he vowed that if he were spared all of them would lose their scalps. A few days afterward the woman became so exhausted that she could walk no farther, so the Illinois slew her. But before she died she extracted a promise from the boy that he would avenge her, and would never cease to be a Seneca.

In a few days they arrived at the Illinois camp, where a council was held to consider the fate of the captive lad. Some were for instantly putting him to death, but their chief ruled that should he be able to live through their tortures he would be worthy of becoming an Illinois. They seized the wretched lad and held his bare feet to the glowing council-fire, then after piercing them they told him to run a race. He bounded forward, and ran so swiftly that he soon gained the Great House of the tribe, where he seated himself upon a wild-cat skin.

Another council was held, and the Illinois braves agreed that the lad possessed high courage and would make a great warrior; but others argued that he knew their warpath and might betray them, and it was finally decided that he should be burnt at the stake. As he was about to perish in this manner an aged warrior suggested that if he were able to withstand their last torture he should be permitted to live. Accordingly he held the unfortunate lad underwater in a pool until only a spark of life remained in him, but he survived, and became an Illinois warrior.

Years passed, and the boy reached manhood and married a chief's daughter. His strength and endurance became proverbial, but the warriors of the tribe of his adoption would never permit him to take part in their warlike expeditions. At length a raid against the Senecas was mooted, and he begged so hard to be allowed to accompany the braves that at last they consented. Indeed, so great was their admiration of the skill with which he outlined a plan of campaign that they made him chief of the expedition. For many days the party marched toward the Seneca country; but when at last they neared it their scouts reported that there were no signs of the tribe, and that the Senecas must have quitted their territory. Their leader, however, proposed to go in search of the enemy himself, along with another warrior of the tribe, and this was agreed to.

When the pair had gone five or six miles the leader said to his companion that it would be better if they separated, as they would then be able to cover more ground. Passing on to where he knew he would find the Senecas, he warned them of their danger, and arranged that an ambush of his kinfolk should lie in wait for the Illinois.

Returning to the Illinois camp, he reported that he had seen nothing, but that he well remembered the Seneca hiding-place. He asked to be given the bravest warriors, and assured the council that he would soon bring them the scalps of their foes. Suspecting nothing, they assented to his proposal, and he was followed by the flower of the Illinois tribe, all unaware that five hundred Senecas awaited them in the valley. The youth led his men right into the heart of the ambush; then, pretending to miss his footing, he fell. This was the signal for the Senecas to rise on every side. Yelling their war cry, they rushed from shelter and fell on the dismayed Illinois, who gave way on every side. The slaughter was immense. Vengeance nerved the arms of the Seneca braves, and of three hundred Illinois but two escaped. The leader of the expedition was borne in triumph to the Seneca village, where to listening hundreds he told the story of his capture and long-meditated revenge. He became a great chief among his people, and even to this day his name is uttered by them with honour and reverence.

THE BOY MAGICIAN

In the heart of the wilderness there lived an old woman and her little grandson. The two found no lack of occupation from day to day, the woman busying herself with cooking and cleaning and the boy with shooting and hunting. The grandmother frequently spoke of the time when the child would grow up and go out into the world.

"Always go to the east," she would say. "Never go to the west, for there lies danger."

But what the danger was she would not tell him, in spite of his importunate questioning. Other boys went west, he thought to himself, and why should not he? Nevertheless his grandmother made him promise that he would not go west.

Years passed by, and the child grew to be a man, though he still retained the curiosity and high spirits of his boyhood. His persistent inquiries drew from the old grandmother a reluctant explanation of her warning.

"In the west," said she, "there dwells a being who is anxious to do us harm. If he sees you it will mean death for both of us."

This statement, instead of frightening the young Indian, only strengthened in him a secret resolution he had formed to go west at the first opportunity. Not that he wished to bring any misfortune on his poor old grandmother, any more than on himself, but he trusted to his strong arm and clear head to deliver them from their enemy. So with a laugh on his lips he set off to the west.

Toward evening he came to a lake, where he rested. He had not been there long when he heard a voice saying: "Aha, my fine fellow, I see you!"

The youth looked all round him, and up into the sky above, but he saw no one.

"I am going to send a hurricane," the mysterious voice continued, "to break your grandmother's hut to pieces. How will you like that?"

"Oh, very well," answered the young man gaily. "We are always in need of firewood, and now we shall have plenty."

"Go home and see," the voice said mockingly. "I daresay you will not like it so well."

Nothing daunted, the young adventurer retraced his steps. As he neared home a great wind sprang up, seeming to tear the very trees out by the roots.

"Make haste!" cried the grandmother from the doorway. "We shall both be killed!"

When she had drawn him inside and shut the door she scolded him heartily for his disobedience, and bewailed the fate before them. The young man soothed her fears, saying: "Don't cry, grandmother. We shall turn the lodge into a rock, and so we shall be saved."

Having some skill in magic, he did as he had said, and the hurrricane passed harmlessly over their heads. When it had ceased they emerged from their retreat, and found an ambulance of firewood all round them.

THE HAILSTORM

Next day the youth was on the point of setting off toward the west once more, but the urgent entreaties of his grandmother moved him to proceed eastward—for a time. Directly he was out of sight of the lodge he turned his face once more to the west. Arrived at the lake, he heard the voice once more, though its owner was still invisible.

"I am going to send a great hailstorm on your grandmother's hut," it said. "What do you think of that?"

"Oh," was the response, "I think I should like it. I have always wanted a bundle of spears."

"Go home and see," said the voice.

Away the youth went through the woods. The sky became darker and darker as he neared his home, and just as he was within a bowshot of the little hut a fierce hailstorm broke, and he thought he would be killed before he reached shelter.

"Alas!" cried the old woman when he was safely indoors, "we shall be destroyed this time. How can we save ourselves?"

Again the young man exercised his magic powers, and transformed the frail hut into a hollow rock, upon which the shafts of the hailstorm spent themselves in vain. At last the sky cleared, the lodge resumed its former shape, and the young man saw a multitude of sharp, beautiful spearheads on the ground.

"I will get poles," said he, "to fit to them for fishing."

When he returned in a few minutes with the poles he found that the spears had vanished.

"Where are my beautiful spears?" he asked his grandmother.

"They were only ice-spears," she replied. "They have all melted away."

The young Indian was greatly disappointed, and wondered how he could avenge himself on the being who had played him this malicious trick.

"Be warned in time," said the aged grandmother, shaking her head at him. "Take my advice and leave him alone."

THE CHARMED STONE

But the youth's adventurous spirit impelled him to see the end of the matter, so he took a stone and tied it round his neck for a charm, and sought the lake once again. Carefully observing the direction from which the voice proceeded, he saw in the middle of the lake a huge head with a face on every side of it.

"Aha! uncle," he exclaimed, "I see you! How would you like it if the lake dried up?"

"Nonsense!" said the voice angrily, "that will never happen."

"Go home and see," shouted the youth, mimicking the mocking tone the other had adopted on the previous occasions. As he spoke he swung his charmed stone round his head and threw it into the air. As it descended it grew larger and larger, and the moment it entered the lake the water began to boil.

The lad returned home and told his grandmother what he had done.

"It is of no use," said she. "Many have tried to slay him, but all have perished in the attempt."

Next morning our hero went westward again, and found the lake quite dry, and the animals in it dead, with the exception of a large green frog, who was in reality the malicious being who had tormented the Indian and his grandmother. A quick blow with a stick put an end to the creature, and the triumphant youth bore the good news to his old grandmother, who from that time was left in peace and quietness.

THE FRIENDLY SKELETON

A little boy living in the woods with his old uncle was warned by him not to go eastward, but to play close to the lodge or walk toward the west. The child felt a natural curiosity to know what lay in the forbidden direction, and one day took advantage of his uncle's absence on a hunting expedition to wander away to the east. At length he came to a large lake, on the shores of which he stopped to rest. Here he was accosted by a man, who asked him his name and where he lived.

"Come," said the stranger, when he had finished questioning the boy, "let us see who can shoot an arrow the highest."

This they did, and the boy's arrow went much higher than that of his companion.

The stranger then suggested a swimming match.

"Let us see," he said, "who can swim farthest under water without taking a breath."

Again the boy beat his rival, who next proposed that they should sail out to an island in the middle of the lake, to see the beautiful birds that were to be found there. The child consented readily, and they embarked in a curious canoe, which was propelled by three swans harnessed to either side of it. Directly they had taken their seats the man began to sing, and the canoe moved off. In a very short time they had reached the island. Here the little Indian realized that his confidence in his new-found friend was misplaced. The stranger took all his clothes from him, put them in the canoe, and jumped in himself, saying:

"Come, swans, let us go home."

The obedient swans set off at a good pace, and soon left the island far behind. The boy was very angry at having been so badly used, but when it grew dark his resentment changed to fear, and he sat down and cried with cold and misery. Suddenly he heard a husky voice close at hand, and, looking round, he saw a skeleton on the ground.

"I am very sorry for you," said the skeleton in hoarse tones. "I will do what I can to help you. But first you must do something for me. Go and dig by that tree, and you shall find a tobacco-pouch with some tobacco in it, a pipe, and a flint."

The boy did as he was asked, and when he had filled the pipe he lit it and placed it in the mouth of the skeleton. He saw that the latter's body was full of mice, and that the smoke frightened them away.

"There is a man coming tonight with three dogs," said the skeleton. "He is coming to look for you. You must make tracks all over the island, so that they may not find you, and then hide in a hollow tree."

Again the boy obeyed his gaunt instructor, and when he was safely hidden he saw a man come ashore with three dogs. All night they hunted him, but he had made so many tracks that the dogs were confused, and at last the man departed in anger. Next day the trembling boy emerged and went to the skeleton.

"To-night," said the latter, "the man who brought you here is coming to drink your blood. You must dig a hole in the sand and hide. When he comes out of the canoe you must enter it. Say, 'Come, swans, let us go home,' and if the man calls you do not look back."

THE LOST SISTER

Everything fell out as the skeleton had foretold. The boy hid in the sand, and directly he saw his tormentor step ashore he jumped into the canoe, saying hastily, "Come, swans, let us go home." Then he began to sing as he had heard the man do when they first embarked. In vain the man

called him back; he refused to look round. The swans carried the canoe
to a cave in a high rock, where the boy found his clothes, as well as a fire
and food. When he had donned his garments and satisfied his hunger he
lay down and slept. In the morning he returned to the island, where he
found the tyrant quite dead. The skeleton now commanded him to sail
eastward to seek for his sister, whom a fierce man had carried away. He
set out eagerly on his new quest, and a three-day journey brought him
to the place where his sister was. He lost no time in finding her.

"Come, my sister," said he, "let us flee together."

"Alas! I cannot," answered the young woman. "A wicked man keeps
me here. It is time for him to return home, and he would be sure to catch
us. But let me hide you now, and in the morning we shall go away."

So she dug a pit and hid her brother, though not a moment too soon,
for the footsteps of her husband were heard approaching the hut. The
woman had cooked a child, and this she placed before the man.

"You have had visitors," he said, seeing his dogs snuffing around uneasily.

"No," was the reply, "I have seen no one but you."

"I shall wait till tomorrow," said the man to himself. "Then I shall kill
and eat him." He had already guessed that his wife had not spoken the
truth. However, he said nothing more, but waited till morning, when,
instead of going to a distant swamp to seek for food, as he pretended to
do, he concealed himself at a short distance from the hut, and at length
saw the brother and sister making for a canoe. They were hardly seated
when they saw him running toward them. In his hand he bore a large
hook, with which he caught the frail vessel; but the lad broke the hook
with a stone, and the canoe darted out on to the lake. The man was at a
loss for a moment, and could only shout incoherent threats after the pair.
Then an idea occurred to him, and, lying down on the shore, he began
to drink the water. This caused the canoe to rush back again, but once
more the boy was equal to the occasion. Seizing the large stone with
which he had broken the hook, he threw it at the man and slew him, the
water at the same time rushing back into the lake. Thus the brother and
sister escaped, and in three days they had arrived at the island, where they
heartily thanked their benefactor, the skeleton. He, however, had still
another task for the young Indian to perform.

"Take your sister home to your uncle's lodge," said he; "then return
here yourself, and say to the many bones which you will find on the
island, 'Arise,' and they shall come to life again."

When the brother and sister reached their home they found that their
old uncle had been grievously lamenting the loss of his nephew, and he
was quite overjoyed at seeing them. On his recommendation they built
a large lodge to accommodate the people they were to bring back with
them. When it was completed, the youth revisited the island, bade the

bones arise, and was delighted to see them obey his bidding and become men and women. He led them to the lodge he had built, where they all dwelt happily for a long time.

THE PIGMIES

When the Cherokees were dwelling in the swamps of Florida the Iroquois made a practice of swooping down on them and raiding their camps. On one occasion the raiding party was absent from home for close on two years. On the eve of their return one of their number, a chieftain, fell ill, and the rest of the party were at a loss to know what to do with him. Obviously, if they carried him home with them he would considerably impede their progress. Besides, there was the possibility that he might not recover, and all their labour would be to no purpose. Thus they debated far into the night, and finally decided to abandon him to his fate and return by themselves. The sick man, unable to stir hand or foot, overheard their decision, but he bore it stoically, like an Indian warrior. Nevertheless, when he heard the last swish of their paddles as they crossed the river he could not help thinking of the friends and kindred he would probably never see again.

When the raiders reached home they were closely questioned as to the whereabouts of the missing chief, and the inquiries were all the more anxious because the sick man had been a great favourite among his people. The guilty warriors answered evasively. They did not know what had become of their comrade, they said. Possibly he had been lost or killed in Florida.

Meanwhile the sick man lay dying on the banks of the river. Suddenly he heard, quite close at hand, the gentle sound of a canoe. The vessel drew in close to the bank, and, in full view of the warrior, three pigmy men disembarked. They regarded the stranger with some surprise. At length one who seemed to be the leader advanced and spoke to him, bidding him await their return, and promising to look after him. They were going, he said, to a certain "salt-lick," where many curious animals watered, in order to kill some for food.

THE SALT-LICK

When the pigmies arrived at the place they found that no animals were as yet to be seen, but very soon a large buffalo bull came to drink. Immediately a buffalo cow arose from the lick, and when they had satisfied their thirst the two animals lay down on the bank. The pigmies concluded that the time was ripe for killing them, and, drawing their bows, they succeeded in dispatching the buffaloes. Returning to the sick man, they amply fulfilled their promise to take care of him, skilfully tending him until he had made a complete recovery. They then conveyed him to his friends, who now learnt that the story told to them by the raiders was false. Bitterly indignant at the deception and heartless cruelty of these men, they fell upon them and punished them according to their deserts.

Later the chief headed a band of people who were curious to see the lick, which they found surrounded by the bones of numberless large animals which had been killed by the pigmies.

This story is interesting as a record of what were perhaps the last vestiges of a pigmy folk who at one time inhabited the eastern portion of North America, before the coming of the Red Man. We have already alluded to this people, in the pages dealing with the discoveries of the Norsemen in the continent.

THE MAGICAL SERPENT

In the seventeenth century a strange legend concerning a huge serpent was found among the Hurons, who probably got it from the neighbouring Algonquins. This monster had on its head a horn which would pierce anything, even the hardest rock. anyone possessing a piece of it was supposed to have very good fortune. The Hurons did not know where the creature was to be found, but said that the Algonquins were in the habit of selling them small pieces of the magic horn.

It is possible that the mercenary Shawnees had borrowed this myth from the Cherokees for their own purposes. At all events a similar legend existed among both tribes which told of a monster snake, the King of Rattlesnakes, who dwelt up among the mountain-passes, attended by a retinue of his kind. Instead of a crown, he wore on his head a beautiful jewel which possessed magic properties. Many a brave tried to obtain possession of this desirable gem, but all fell victims to the venomous reptiles. At length a more ingenious warrior clothed himself entirely in leather, and so rendered himself impervious to their attack. Making his way to the haunt of the serpents, he slew their monster chief. Then, triumphantly taking possession of the wonderful jewel, he bore it to his tribe, by whom it was regarded with profound veneration and jealously preserved.

THE ORIGIN OF MEDICINE

An interesting Cherokee myth is that which recounts the origin of disease, and the consequent institution of curative medicine. In the old days, we are told, the members of the brute creation were gifted with speech and dwelt in amity with the human race, but mankind multiplied so quickly that the animals were crowded into the forests and desert places of the earth, so that the old friendship between them was soon forgotten. The breach was farther widened by the invention of lethal weapons, by the aid of which man commenced the wholesale slaughter of the beasts for the sake of their flesh and skins. The animals, at first surprised, soon grew angry, and resolved upon measures of retaliation. The bear tribe met in council, presided over by the Old White Bear, their chief. After several speakers had denounced mankind for their bloodthirsty tendencies, war was unanimously decided upon, but the lack of weapons was regarded as a serious drawback. However, it was suggested that man's instruments should be turned against himself, and as the bow and arrow were considered to be the principal human agency of destruction, it was resolved to fashion a specimen. A suitable piece of wood was procured, and one of the bears sacrificed himself to provide gut for a bowstring. When the weapon was completed it was discovered that the claws of the bears spoiled their shooting. One of the bears, however, cut his claws, and succeeded in hitting the mark, but the Old White Bear very wisely remarked that without claws they could not climb trees or bring down game, and that were they to cut them off they must all starve.

The deer also met in council, under their chief, the Little Deer, when it was decided that those hunters who slew one of their number without asking pardon in a suitable manner should be afflicted with rheumatism. They gave notice of this decision to the nearest settlement of Indians, and instructed them on how to make propitiation when forced by necessity to kill one of the deer-folk. So when a deer is slain by the hunter the Little Deer runs to the spot, and, bending over the bloodstains, asks the spirit of the deer if it has heard the prayer of the hunter for pardon. If the reply be "Yes," all is well, and the Little Deer departs; but if the answer be in the negative, he tracks the hunter to his cabin, and strikes him with rheumatism, so that he becomes a helpless cripple. Sometimes hunters who have not learned the proper formula for pardon attempt to turn aside the Little Deer from his pursuit by building a fire behind them in the trail.

THE COUNCIL OF THE FISHES

The fishes and reptiles then held a joint council, and arranged to haunt those human beings who tormented them with hideous dreams of serpents twining round them and of eating fish which had become decayed. These snake and fish dreams seem to be of common occurrence among the Cherokees, and the services of the *shamans* to banish them are in constant demand.

Lastly, the birds and the insects, with the smaller animals, gathered together for a similar purpose, the grub-worm presiding over the meeting. Each in turn expressed an opinion, and the consensus was against mankind. They devised and named various diseases.

When the plants, which were friendly to man, heard what had been arranged by the animals, they determined to frustrate their evil designs. Each tree, shrub, and herb, down even to the grasses and mosses, agreed to furnish a remedy for someone of the diseases named. Thus did medicine come into being. When the *shaman* is in doubt as to what treatment to apply for the relief of a patient the spirit of the plant suggests a fitting remedy.

THE WONDERFUL KETTLE

A story is told among the Iroquois of two brothers who lived in the wilderness far from all human habitation. The elder brother went into the forest to hunt game, while the younger stayed at home and tended the hut, cooked the food, and gathered firewood.

One evening the tired hunter returned from the chase, and the younger brother took the game from him as usual and dressed it for supper. "I will smoke awhile before I eat," said the hunter, and he smoked in silence for a time. When he was tired of smoking he lay down and went to sleep.

"Strange," said the boy; "I should have thought he would want to eat first."

When the hunter awoke he found that his brother had prepared the supper and was waiting for him.

"Go to bed," said he; "I wish to be alone."

Wondering much, the boy did as he was bidden, but he could not help asking himself how his brother could possibly live if he did not eat. In the morning he observed that the hunter went away without tasting any food, and on many succeeding mornings and evenings the same thing happened.

"I must watch him at night," said the boy to himself, "for he must eat at night, since he eats at no other time."

That same evening, when the lad was told as usual to go to bed, he lay down and pretended to be sound asleep, but all the time one of his eyes was open. In this cautious fashion he watched his brother, and saw him rise from his couch and pass through a trapdoor in the floor, from which he shortly emerged bearing a rusty kettle, the bottom of which he scraped industriously. Filling it with water, he set it on the blazing fire. As he did so he struck it with a whip, saying at every blow: "Grow larger, my kettle!"

The obedient kettle became of gigantic proportions, and after setting it aside to cool the man ate its contents with evident relish.

His watchful younger brother, well content with the result of his observations, turned over and went to sleep.

When the elder had set off next morning, the boy, filled with curiosity, opened the trapdoor and discovered the kettle. "I wonder what he eats," he said, and there within the vessel was half a chestnut! He was rather surprised at this discovery, but he thought to himself how pleased

his brother would be if on his return he found a meal to his taste awaiting him. When evening drew near he put the kettle on the fire, took a
whip, and, hitting it repeatedly, exclaimed: "Grow larger, my kettle!"

The kettle grew larger, but to the boy's alarm it kept on growing until
it filled the room, and he was obliged to get on the roof and stir it
through the chimney.

"What are you doing up there?" shouted the hunter, when he came
within hail.

"I took your kettle to get your supper ready," answered the boy.

"Alas!" cried the other, "now I must die!"

He quickly reduced the kettle to its original proportions and put it in
its place. But he still wore such a sad and serious air that his brother was
filled with dismay, and prayed that he might be permitted to undo the mischief he had wrought. When the days went past and he found that his
brother no longer went out to hunt or displayed any interest in life, but
grew gradually thinner and more melancholy, his distress knew no bounds.

"Let me fetch you some chestnuts," he begged earnestly. "Tell me
where they may be found."

THE WHITE HERON

"You must travel a full day's journey," said the hunter in response to his
entreaties. "You will then reach a river which is most difficult to ford.
On the opposite bank there stands a lodge, and near by a chestnut-tree.
Even then your difficulties will only be begun. The tree is guarded by a
white heron, which never loses sight of it for a moment. He is employed
for that purpose by the six women who live in the lodge, and with their
war-clubs they slay anyone who has the temerity to approach. I beg of
you, do not think of going on such a hopeless errand."

But the boy felt that were the chance of success even more slender he
must make the attempt for the sake of his brother, whom his thought-
lessness had brought low.

He made a little canoe about three inches long, and set off on his journey, in the direction indicated by his brother. At the end of a day he came
to the river, whose size had not been underestimated. Taking his little
canoe from his pocket, he drew it out till it was of a suitable length, and
launched it in the great stream. A few minutes sufficed to carry him to
the opposite bank, and there he beheld the lodge and the chestnut-tree.
On his way he had managed to procure some seeds of a sort greatly liked
by herons, and these he scattered before the beautiful white bird strutting
round the tree. While the heron was busily engaged in picking them up
the young man seized his opportunity and gathered quantities of the
chestnuts, which were lying thickly on the ground. Ere his task was finished, however, the heron perceived the intruder, and called a loud warn-

ing to the women in the lodge, who were not slow to respond. They rushed out with their fishing-lines in their hands, and gave chase to the thief. But fear, for his brother as well as for himself, lent the youth wings, and he was well out on the river in his canoe when the shrieking women reached the bank. The eldest threw her line and caught him, but with a sharp pull he broke it. Another line met with the same fate, and so on, until all the women had thrown their lines. They could do nothing further, and were obliged to watch the retreating canoe in impotent rage.

At length the youth, having come safely through the perils of the journey, arrived home with his precious burden of chestnuts. He found his brother still alive, but so weak that he could hardly speak. A meal of the chestnuts, however, helped to revive him, and he quickly recovered.

THE STONE GIANTESS

In bygone times it was customary for a hunter's wife to accompany her husband when he sought the chase. A dutiful wife on these occasions would carry home the game killed by the hunter and dress and cook it for him.

There was once a chief among the Iroquois who was a very skilful hunter. In all his expeditions his wife was his companion and helper. On one excursion he found such large quantities of game that he built a wigwam at the place, and settled there for a time with his wife and child. One day he struck out on a new track, while his wife followed the path they had taken on the previous day, in order to gather the game killed then. As the woman turned her steps homeward after a hard day's work she heard the sound of another woman's voice inside the hut. Filled with surprise, she entered, but found to her consternation that her visitor was no other than a Stone Giantess. To add to her alarm, she saw that the creature had in her arms the chief's baby. While the mother stood in the doorway, wondering how she could rescue her child from the clutches of the giantess, the latter said in a gentle and soothing voice: "Do not be afraid: come inside."

The hunter's wife hesitated no longer, but boldly entered the wigwam. Once inside, her fear changed to pity, for the giantess was evidently much worn with trouble and fatigue. She told the hunter's wife, who was kindly and sympathetic, how she had travelled from the land of the Stone Giants, fleeing from her cruel husband, who had sought to kill her, and how she had finally taken shelter in the solitary wigwam. She besought the young woman to let her remain for a while, promising to assist her in her daily tasks. She also said she was very hungry, but warned her hostess that she must be exceedingly careful about the food she gave her. It must not be raw or at all underdone, for if once she tasted blood she might wish to kill the hunter and his wife and child.

So the wife prepared some food for her, taking care that it was thoroughly cooked, and the two sat down to dine together. The Stone Giantess knew that the woman was in the habit of carrying home the game, and she now declared that she would do it in her stead. Moreover, she said she already knew where it was to be found, and insisted on setting out for it at once. She very shortly returned, bearing in one hand a load of game which four men could scarcely have carried, and the woman recognized in her a very valuable assistant.

The time of the hunter's return drew near, and the Stone Giantess bade the wife go out and meet her husband and tell him of her visitor. The man was very well pleased to learn how the newcomer had helped his wife, and he gave her a hearty welcome. In the morning he went out hunting as usual. When he had disappeared from sight in the forest the giantess turned quickly to the woman and said:

"I have a secret to tell you. My cruel husband is after me, and in three days he will arrive here. On the third day your husband must remain at home and help me to slay him."

When the third day came round the hunter remained at home, obedient to the instructions of his guest.

"Now," said the giantess at last, "I hear him coming. You must both help me to hold him. Strike him where I bid you, and we shall certainly kill him."

The hunter and his wife were seized with terror when a great commotion outside announced the arrival of the Stone Giant, but the firmness and courage of the giantess reassured them, and with something like calmness they awaited the monster's approach. Directly he came in sight the giantess rushed forward, grappled with him and threw him to the ground.

"Strike him on the arms!" she cried to the others. "Now on the nape of the neck!"

The trembling couple obeyed, and very shortly they had succeeded in killing the huge creature.

"I will go and bury him," said the giantess. And that was the end of the Stone Giant.

The strange guest stayed on in the wigwam till the time came for the hunter and his family to go back to the settlement, when she announced her intention of returning to her own people.

"My husband is dead," said she; "I no longer have anything to fear." Thus, having bade them farewell, she departed.

THE HEALING WATERS

The Iroquois have a touching story of how a brave of their race once saved his wife and his people from extinction.

It was winter, the snow lay thickly on the ground, and there was sorrow in the encampment, for with the cold weather a dreadful plague had visited the people. There was not one but had lost some relative, and in some cases whole families had been swept away. Among those who had been most sorely bereaved was Nekumonta, a handsome young brave, whose parents, brothers, sisters, and children had died one by one before his eyes, the while he was powerless to help them. And now his wife, the beautiful Shanewis, was weak and ill. The dreaded disease had laid its awful finger on her brow, and she knew that she must shortly bid her husband farewell and take her departure for the place of the dead. Already she saw her dead friends beckoning her and inviting her to join them, but it grieved her terribly to think that she must leave her young husband in sorrow and loneliness. His despair was piteous to behold when she broke the sad news to him, but after the first outburst of grief he bore up bravely, and determined to fight the plague with all his strength.

"I must find the healing herbs which the Great Manitou has planted," said he. "Wherever they may be, I must find them."

So he made his wife comfortable on her couch, covering her with warm furs, and then, embracing her gently, he set out on his difficult mission.

All day he sought eagerly in the forest for the healing herbs, but everywhere the snow lay deep, and not so much as a blade of grass was visible. When night came he crept along the frozen ground, thinking that his sense of smell might aid him in his search. Thus for three days and nights he wandered through the forest, over hills and across rivers, in a vain attempt to discover the means of curing the malady of Shanewis.

When he met a little scurrying rabbit in the path he cried eagerly: "Tell me, where shall I find the herbs which Manitou has planted?"

But the rabbit hurried away without reply, for he knew that the herbs had not yet risen above the ground, and he was very sorry for the brave.

Nekumonta came by and by to the den of a big bear, and of this animal also he asked the same question. But the bear could give him no reply, and he was obliged to resume his weary journey. He consulted all the beasts of the forest in turn, but from none could he get any help. How could they tell him, indeed, that his search was hopeless?

THE PITY OF THE TREES

On the third night he was very weak and ill, for he had tasted no food since he had first set out, and he was numbed with cold and despair. He stumbled over a withered branch hidden under the snow, and so tired was he that he lay where he fell, and immediately went to sleep. All the birds and the beasts, all the multitude of creatures that inhabit the forest, came to watch over his slumbers. They remembered his kindness to them in former days, how he had never slain an animal unless he really needed it for food or clothing, how he had loved and protected the trees and the flowers. Their hearts were touched by his courageous fight for Shanewis, and they pitied his misfortunes. All that they could do to aid him they did. They cried to the Great Manitou to save his wife from the plague which held her, and the Great Spirit heard the manifold whispering and responded to their prayers.

While Nekumonta lay asleep there came to him the messenger of Manitou, and he dreamed. In his dream he saw his beautiful Shanewis, pale and thin, but as lovely as ever, and as he looked she smiled at him, and sang a strange, sweet song, like the murmuring of a distant waterfall. Then the scene changed, and it really was a waterfall he heard. In musical language it called him by name, saying: "Seek us, O Nekumonta, and when you find us Shanewis shall live. We are the Healing Waters of the Great Manitou."

Nekumonta awoke with the words of the song still ringing in his ears. Starting to his feet, he looked in every direction; but there was no water to be seen, though the murmuring sound of a waterfall was distinctly audible. He fancied he could even distinguish words in it.

THE FINDING OF THE WATERS

"Release us!" it seemed to say. "Set us free, and Shanewis shall be saved!" Nekumonta searched in vain for the waters. Then it suddenly occurred to him that they must be underground, directly under his feet. Seizing branches, stones, flints, he dug feverishly into the earth. So arduous was the task that before it was finished he was completely exhausted. But at last the hidden spring was disclosed, and the waters were rippling merrily down the vale, carrying life and happiness wherever they went. The young man bathed his aching limbs in the healing stream, and in a moment he was well and strong.

Raising his hands, he gave thanks to Manitou. With eager fingers he made a jar of clay, and baked it in the fire, so that he might carry life to Shanewis. As he pursued his way homeward with his treasure his despair was changed to rejoicing and he sped like the wind.

When he reached his village his companions ran to greet him. Their faces were sad and hopeless, for the plague still raged. However, Nekumonta directed them to the Healing Waters and inspired them with new hope. Shanewis he found on the verge of the Shadow-land, and scarcely able to murmur a farewell to her husband. But Nekumonta did not listen to her broken adieux. He forced some of the Healing Water between her parched lips, and bathed her hands and her brow till she fell into a gentle slumber. When she awoke the fever had left her, she was serene and smiling, and Nekumonta's heart was filled with a great happiness.

The tribe was forever rid of the dreaded plague, and the people gave to Nekumonta the title of "Chief of the Healing Waters," so that all might know that it was he who had brought them the gift of Manitou.

SAYADIO IN SPIRIT-LAND

A legend of the Wyandot tribe of the Iroquois relates how Sayadio, a young Indian, mourned greatly for a beautiful sister who had died young. So deeply did he grieve for her that at length he resolved to seek her in the Land of Spirits. Long he sought the maiden, and many adventures did he meet with. Years passed in the search, which he was about to abandon as wholly in vain, when he encountered an old man, who gave him some good advice. This venerable person also bestowed upon him a magic calabash in which he might catch and retain the spirit of his sister should he succeed in finding her. He afterward discovered that this old man was the keeper of that part of the Spirit-land which he sought.

Delighted to have achieved so much, Sayadio pursued his way, and in due time reached the Land of Souls. But to his dismay he perceived that the spirits, instead of advancing to meet him as he had expected, fled from him in terror. Greatly dejected, he approached Tarenyawago, the spirit master of ceremonies, who took compassion upon him and informed him that the dead had gathered together for a great dance festival, just such as the Indians themselves celebrate at certain seasons of the year. Soon the dancing commenced, and Sayadio saw the spirits floating round in a mazy measure like wreaths of mist. Among them he perceived his sister, and sprang forward to embrace her, but she eluded his grasp and dissolved into air.

Much cast down, the youth once more appealed to the sympathetic master of ceremonies, who gave him a magic rattle of great power, by the sound of which he might bring her back. Again the spirit-music sounded for the dance, and the dead folk thronged into the circle. Once more Sayadio saw his sister, and observed that she was so wholly entranced with the music that she took no heed of his presence. Quick as thought the young Indian dipped up the ghost with his calabash as one nets a fish, and secured the cover, in spite of all the efforts of the captured soul to regain its liberty.

Retracing his steps earthward, he had no difficulty in making his way back to his native village, where he summoned his friends to come and behold his sister's resuscitation. The girl's corpse was brought from its resting place to be reanimated with its spirit, and all was prepared for the ceremony, when a witless Indian maiden must needs peep into the calabash in her curiosity to see how a disembodied spirit looked. Instantly, as a bird rises when its cage bars are opened and flies forth to freedom, the spirit of Sayadio's sister flew from the calabash before the startled youth could dash forward and shut down the cover. For a while Sayadio could not realize his loss, but at length his straining eyes revealed to him that the spirit of his sister was not within sight. In a flash he saw the ruin of his hopes, and with a broken heart he sank senseless to the earth.

THE PEACE QUEEN

A brave of the Oneida tribe of the Iroquois hunted in the forest. The red buck flashed past him, but not swifter than his arrow, for as the deer leaped he loosed his shaft and it pierced the dappled hide.

The young man strode toward the carcass, knife in hand, but as he seized the horns the branches parted, and the angry face of an Onondaga warrior lowered between them.

"Leave the buck, Oneida," he commanded fiercely. "It is the spoil of my bow. I wounded the beast ere you saw it."

The Oneida laughed. "My brother may have shot at the buck," he said, "but what avails that if he did not slay it?"

"The carcass is mine by right of forest law," cried the other in a rage. "Will you quit it or will you fight?"

The Oneida drew himself up and regarded the Onondaga scornfully.

"As my brother pleases," he replied. Next moment the two were locked in a life-and-death struggle.

Tall was the Onondaga and strong as a great tree of the forest. The Oneida, lithe as a panther, fought with all the courage of youth. To and fro they swayed, till their breathing came thick and fast and the falling sweat blinded their eyes. At length they could struggle no longer, and by a mutual impulse they sprang apart.

THE QUARREL

"Ho! Onondaga," cried the younger man, "what profits it thus to strive for a buck? Is there no meat in the lodges of your people that they must fight for it like the mountain lion?"

"Peace, young man!" retorted the grave Onondaga. "I had not fought for the buck had not your evil tongue roused me. But I am older than you, and, I trust, wiser. Let us seek the lodge of the Peace Queen hard by, and she will award the buck to him who has the best right to it."

"It is well," said the Oneida, and side by side they sought the lodge of the Peace Queen.

Now the Five Nations in their wisdom had set apart a Seneca maiden dwelling alone in the forest as arbiter of quarrels between braves. This maiden the men of all tribes regarded as sacred and as apart from other women. Like the ancient Vestals, she could not become the bride of any man.

As the Peace Queen heard the wrathful clamour of the braves outside her lodge she stepped forth, little pleased that they should thus profane the vicinity of her dwelling.

"Peace!" she cried. "If you have a grievance enter and state it. It is not fitting that braves should quarrel where the Peace Queen dwells."

At her words the men stood abashed. They entered the lodge and told the story of their meeting and the circumstances of their quarrel.

When they had finished the Peace Queen smiled scornfully. "So two such braves as you can quarrel about a buck?" she said. "Go, Onondaga, as the elder, and take one half of the spoil, and bear it back to your wife and children."

But the Onondaga stood his ground.

THE OFFERS

"O Queen," he said, "my wife is in the Land of Spirits, snatched from me by the Plague Demon. But my lodge does not lack food. I would wive again, and thine eyes have looked into my heart as the sun pierces the darkness of the forest. Will you come to my lodge and cook my venison?"

But the Peace Queen shook her head.

"You know that the Five Nations have placed Genetaska apart to be Peace Queen," she replied firmly, "and that her vows may not be broken. Go in peace."

The Onondaga was silent.

Then spoke the Oneida. "O Peace Queen," he said, gazing steadfastly at Genetaska, whose eyes dropped before his glance, "I know that you are set apart by the Five Nations. But it is in my mind to ask you to go with me to my lodge, for I love you. What says Genetaska?"

The Peace Queen blushed and answered: "To you also I say, go in peace," but her voice was a whisper which ended in a stifled sob.

The two warriors departed, good friends now that they possessed a common sorrow. But the Peace Maiden had forever lost her peace. For she could not forget the young Oneida brave, so tall, so strong, and so gentle.

Summer darkened into autumn, and autumn whitened into winter. Warriors innumerable came to the Peace Lodge for the settlement of disputes. Outwardly Genetaska was calm and untroubled, but though she gave solace to others her own breast could find none.

One day she sat by the lodge fire, which had burned down to a heap of cinders. She was thinking, dreaming of the young Oneida. Her thoughts

went out to him as birds fly southward to seek the sun. Suddenly a crack-
ling of twigs under a firm step roused her from her reverie. Quickly she
glanced upward. Before her stood the youth of her dreams, pale and
worn.

"Peace Queen," he said sadly, "you have brought darkness to the soul
of the Oneida. No longer may he follow the hunt. The deer may sport
in quiet for him. No longer may he bend the bow or throw the toma-
hawk in contest, or listen to the tale during the long nights round the
campfire. You have his heart in your keeping. Say, will you not give him
yours?"

Softly the Peace Queen murmured: "I will."

Hand in hand like two joyous children they sought his canoe, which
bore them swiftly westward. No longer was Genetaska Peace Queen, for
her vows were broken by the power of love.

The two were happy. But not so for the men of the Five Nations.
They were wroth because the Peace Queen had broken her vows, and
knew how foolish they had been to trust to the word of a young and
beautiful woman. So with one voice they abolished the office of Peace
Queen, and war and tumult returned once more to their own.

III

SIOUX MYTHS AND LEGENDS

THE SIOUX OR DAKOTA INDIANS

THE SIOUX or Dakota Indians dwell north of the Arkansas River on the right bank of the Mississippi, stretching over to Lake Michigan and up the valley of the Missouri. One of their principal tribes is the Iowa.

THE ADVENTURES OF ICTINIKE

Many tales are told by the Iowa Indians regarding Ictinike, the son of the sun-god, who had offended his father, and was consequently expelled from the celestial regions. He possesses a very bad reputation among the Indians for deceit and trickery. They say that he taught them all the evil things they know, and they seem to regard him as a Father of Lies. The Omahas state that he gave them their war-customs, and for one reason or another they appear to look upon him as a species of war-god. A series of myths recount his adventures with several inhabitants of the wild. The first of these is as follows.

One day Ictinike encountered the Rabbit, and hailed him in a friendly manner, calling him "grandchild," and requesting him to do him a service. The Rabbit expressed his willingness to assist the god to the best of his ability, and inquired what he wished him to do.

"Oh, grandchild," said the crafty one, pointing upward to where a bird circled in the blue vault above them, "take your bow and arrow and bring down yonder bird."

The Rabbit fitted an arrow to his bow, and the shaft transfixed the bird, which fell like a stone and lodged in the branches of a great tree.

"Now, grandchild," said Ictinike, "go into the tree and fetch me the game."

This, however, the Rabbit at first refused to do, but at length he took off his clothes and climbed into the tree, where he stuck fast among the tortuous branches.

Ictinike, seeing that he could not make his way down, donned the

81

unfortunate Rabbit's garments, and, highly amused at the animal's predicament, betook himself to the nearest village. There he encountered a chief who had two beautiful daughters, the elder of whom he married. The younger daughter, regarding this as an affront to her personal attractions, wandered off into the forest in a fit of sulks. As she paced angrily up and down she heard someone calling to her from above, and, looking upward, she beheld the unfortunate Rabbit, whose fur was adhering to the natural gum which exuded from the bark of the tree. The girl cut down the tree and lit a fire near it, which melted the gum and freed the Rabbit. The Rabbit and the chief's daughter compared notes, and discovered that the being who had tricked the one and affronted the other was the same. Together they proceeded to the chief's lodge, where the girl was laughed at because of the strange companion she had brought back with her. Suddenly an eagle appeared in the air above them. Ictinike shot at and missed it, but the Rabbit loosed an arrow with great force and brought it to earth. Each morning a feather of the bird became another eagle, and each morning Ictinike shot at and missed this newly created bird, which the Rabbit invariably succeeded in killing. This went on until Ictinike had quite worn out the Rabbit's clothing and was wearing a very old piece of tent skin; but the Rabbit returned to him the garments he had been forced to don when Ictinike had stolen this. Then the Rabbit commanded the Indians to beat the drums, and each time they were beaten Ictinike jumped so high that every bone in his body was shaken. At length, after a more than usually loud series of beats, he leapt to such a height that when he came down it was found that the fall had broken his neck. The Rabbit was avenged.

ICTINIKE AND THE BUZZARD

One day Ictinike, footsore and weary, encountered a buzzard, which he asked to oblige him by carrying him on its back part of the way. The crafty bird immediately consented, and, seating Ictinike between its wings, flew off with him.

They had not gone far when they passed above a hollow tree, and Ictinike began to shift uneasily in his seat as he observed the buzzard hovering over it. He requested the bird to fly onward, but for answer it cast him headlong into the tree-trunk, where he found himself a prisoner. For a long time he lay there in want and wretchedness, until at last a large hunting-party struck camp at the spot. Ictinike changed to be wearing some raccoon skins, and he thrust the tails of these through the cracks in the tree. Three women who were standing near imagined that a number of racoons had become imprisoned in the hollow trunk, and they made a large hole in it for the purpose of capturing them.

Ictinike at once emerged, whereupon the women fled. Ictinike lay on the ground pretending to be dead, and as he was covered with the raccoon-skins the birds of prey, the eagle, the rook, and the magpie, came to devour him. While they pecked at him the buzzard made his appearance for the purpose of joining in the feast, but Ictinike, rising quickly, tore the feathers from its scalp. That is why the buzzard has no feathers on its head.

ICTINIKE AND THE CREATORS

In course of time Ictinike married and dwelt in a lodge of his own. One day he intimated to his wife that it was his intention to visit her grandfather the Beaver. On arriving at the Beaver's lodge he found that his grandfather-in-law and his family had been without food for a long time, and were slowly dying of starvation. Ashamed at having no food to place before their guest, one of the young beavers offered himself up to provide a meal for Ictinike, and was duly cooked and served to the visitor. Before Ictinike partook of the dish, however, he was earnestly requested by the Beaver not to break any of the bones of his son, but unwittingly he split one of the toe-bones. Having finished his repast, he lay down to rest, and the Beaver gathered the bones and put them in a skin. This he plunged into the river that flowed beside his lodge, and in a moment the young beaver emerged from the water alive.

"How do you feel, my son?" asked the Beaver.

"Alas! father," replied the young beaver, "one of my toes is broken."

From that time every beaver has had one toe—that next to the little one—which looks as if it had been split by biting.

Ictinike shortly after took his leave of the Beavers, and pretended to forget his tobacco-pouch, which he left behind. The Beaver told one of his young ones to run after him with the pouch, but, being aware of Ictinike's treacherous character, he advised his offspring to throw it to the god when at some distance away. The young beaver accordingly took the pouch and hurried after Ictinike, and, obeying his father's instruction, was about to throw it to him from a considerable distance when Ictinike called to him: "Come closer, come closer."

The young beaver obeyed, and as Ictinike took the pouch from him he said: "Tell your father that he must visit me."

When the young beaver arrived home he acquainted his father with what had passed, and the Beaver showed signs of great annoyance.

"I knew he would say that," he growled, "and that is why I did not want you to go near him."

But the Beaver could not refuse the invitation, and in due course returned the visit. Ictinike, wishing to pay him a compliment, was about to kill one of his own children wherewith to regale the Beaver, and was slapping it to make it cry in order that he might work himself into a passion sufficiently murderous to enable him to take its life, when the Beaver spoke to him sharply and told him that such a sacrifice was unnecessary. Going down to the stream hard by, the Beaver found a young beaver by the water, which was brought up to the lodge, killed and cooked, and duly eaten.

On another occasion Ictinike announced to his wife his intention of calling upon her grandfather the Muskrat. At the Muskrat's lodge he met with the same tale of starvation as at the home of the Beaver, but the Muskrat told his wife to fetch some water, put it in the kettle, and hang the kettle over the fire. When the water was boiling the Muskrat upset the kettle, which was found to be full of wild rice, upon which Ictinike feasted. As before, he left his tobacco-pouch with his host, and the Muskrat sent one of his children after him with the article. An invitation for the Muskrat to visit him resulted, and the call was duly paid. Ictinike, wishing to display his magical powers, requested his wife to hang a kettle of water over the fire, but, to his chagrin, when the water was boiled and the kettle upset instead of wild rice only water poured out. Thereupon the Muskrat had the kettle refilled, and produced an abundance of rice, much to Ictinike's annoyance.

Ictinike then called upon his wife's grandfather the Kingfisher, who, to provide him with food, dived into the river and brought up fish. Ictinike extended a similar invitation to him, and the visit was duly paid. Desiring to be even with his late host, the god dived into the river in search of fish. He soon found himself in difficulties, however, and if it had not been for the Kingfisher he would most assuredly have been drowned.

Lastly, Ictinike went to visit his wife's grandfather the Flying Squirrel. The Squirrel climbed to the top of his lodge and brought down a quantity of excellent black walnuts, which Ictinike ate. When he departed from the Squirrel's house he purposely left one of his gloves, which a small squirrel brought after him, and he sent an invitation by this messenger for the Squirrel to visit him in turn. Wishing to show his cleverness, Ictinike scrambled to the top of his lodge, but instead of finding any black walnuts thee he fell and severely injured himself. Thus his presumption was punished for the fourth time.

The four beings alluded to in this story as the Beaver, Muskrat, Kingfisher, and Flying Squirrel are four of the creative gods of the Sioux, whom Ictinike evidently could not equal so far as reproductive magic was concerned.

THE STORY OF WABASKAHA

An interesting story is that of Wabaskaha, an Omaha brave, the facts related in which occurred about a century ago. A party of Pawnees on the warpath raided the horses belonging to some Omahas dwelling beside Omaha Creek. Most of the animals were the property of Wabaskaha, who immediately followed on their trail. A few Omahas who had tried to rescue the horses had also been carried off, and on the arrival of the Pawnee party at the Republican River several of the Pawnees proposed to put their prisoners to death. Others, however, refused to participate in such an act, and strenuously opposed the suggestion. A wife of one of the Pawnee chiefs fed the captives, after which her husband gave them permission to depart.

After this incident quite a feeling of friendship sprang up between the two peoples, and the Pawnees were continually inviting the Omahas to feasts and other entertainments, but they refused to return the horses they had stolen. They told Wabaskaha that if he came for his horses in the fall they would exchange them then for a certain amount of gunpowder, and that was the best arrangement he could come to with them. On his way homeward Wabaskaha mourned loudly for the horses, which constituted nearly the whole of his worldly possessions, and called upon Wakanda, his god, to assist and avenge him. In glowing language he recounted the circumstances of his loss to the people of his tribe, and so strong was their sense of the injustice done him that next day a general meeting was held in the village to consider his case. A pipe was filled, and Wabaskaha asked the men of his tribe to place it to their lips if they decided to take vengeance on the Pawnees. All did so, but the premeditated raid was postponed until the early autumn.

After a summer of hunting the braves sought the warpath. They had hardly started when a number of Dakotas arrived at their village, bringing some tobacco. The Dakotas announced their intention of joining the Omaha war-party, the trail of which they took up accordingly. In a few days the Omahas arrived at the Pawnee village, which they attacked at daylight. After a vigorous defence the Pawnees were almost exterminated, and all their horses captured. The Dakotas who had elected to assist the Omaha war-party were, however, slain to a man. Such was the vengeance of Wabaskaha.

This story is interesting as an account of a veritable Indian raid, taken from the lips of Joseph La Flèche, a Dakota Indian.

THE MEN-SERPENTS

Twenty warriors who had been on the warpath were returning homeward worn-out and hungry, and as they went they scattered in search of game to sustain them on their way.

Suddenly one of the braves, placing his ear to the ground, declared that he could hear a herd of buffaloes approaching.

The band was greatly cheered by this news, and the plans made by the chief to intercept the animals were quickly carried into effect.

Nearer and nearer came the supposed herd. The chief lay very still, ready to shoot when it came within range. Suddenly he saw, to his horror, that what approached them was a huge snake with a rattle as large as a man's head. Though almost paralysed with surprise and terror, he managed to shoot the monster and kill it. He called up his men, who were not a little afraid of the gigantic creature, even though it was dead, and for a long time they debated what they should do with the carcass. At length hunger conquered their scruples and made them decide to cook and eat it. To their surprise, they found the meat as savoury as that of a buffalo, which it much resembled. All partook of the fare, with the exception of one boy, who persisted in refusing it, though they pressed him to eat.

When the warriors had finished their meal they lay down beside the campfire and fell asleep. Later in the night the chief awoke and was horrified to find that his companions had turned to snakes, and that he himself was already half snake, half man. Hastily he gathered his transformed warriors, and they saw that the boy who had not eaten of the reptile had retained his own form. The lad, fearing that the serpents might attack him, began to weep, but the snake-warriors treated him very kindly, giving him their charms and all they possessed.

At their request he put them into a large robe and carried them to the summit of a high hill, where he set them down under the trees.

"You must return to our lodges," they told him, "and in the summer we will visit our kindred. See that our wives and children come out to greet us."

The boy carried the news to his village, and there was much weeping and lamentation when the friends of the warriors heard of their fate. But in the summer the snakes came and sat in a group outside the village, and all the people crowded round them, loudly venting their grief. The horses which had belonged to the snakes were brought out to them, as well as their moccasins, leggings, whips, and saddles.

"Do not be afraid of them," said the boy to the assembled people. "Do not flee from them, lest something happens to you also." So they let the snakes creep over them, and no harm befell.

In the winter the snakes vanished altogether, and with them their horses and other possessions, and the people never saw them more.

THE THREE TESTS

There dwelt in a certain village a woman of remarkable grace and attractiveness. The fame of her beauty drew suitors from far and near, eager to display their prowess and win the love of this imperious creature—for, besides being beautiful, she was extremely hard to please, and set such tests for her lovers as none had ever been able to satisfy.

A certain young man who lived at a considerable distance had heard of her great charms, and made up his mind to woo and win her. The difficulty of the task did not daunt him, and full of hope, he set out on his mission.

As he travelled he came to a very high hill, and on the summit he saw a man rising and sitting down at short intervals. When the prospective suitor drew nearer he observed that the man was fastening large stones to his ankles. The youth approached him, saying: "Why do you tie these great stones to your ankles?"

"Oh," replied the other, "I wish to chase buffaloes, and yet whenever I do so I go beyond them, so I am tying stones to my ankles that I may not run so fast."

"My friend," said the suitor, "you can run some other time. In the meantime I am without a companion: come with me."

The Swift One agreed, and they walked on their way together. Ere they had gone very far they saw two large lakes. By the side of one of them sat a man, who frequently bowed his head to the water and drank. Surprised that his thirst was not quenched, they said to him: "Why do you sit there drinking the lake?"

"I can never get enough water. When I have finished this lake I shall start on the other."

"My friend," said the suitor, "do not trouble to drink it just now. Come and join us."

The Thirsty One complied, and the three comrades journeyed on. When they had gone a little farther they noticed a man walking along with his face lifted to the sky. Curious to know why he acted thus, they addressed him.

"Why do you walk with your eyes turned skyward?" said they.

"I have shot an arrow," he said, "and I am waiting for it to reappear."

"Never mind your arrow," said the suitor. "Come with us."

"I will come," said the Skilful Archer.

As the four companions journeyed through a forest they beheld a strange sight. A man was lying with his ear to the ground, and if he lifted his head for a moment he bowed it again, listening intently. The four approached him, saying: "Friend, for what do you listen so earnestly?"

"I am listening," said he, "to the plants growing. This forest is full of plants, and I am listening to their breathing."

"You can listen when the occasion arises," they told him. "Come and join us."

He agreed, and so they travelled to the village where dwelt the beautiful maiden.

When they had reached their destination they were quickly surrounded by the villagers, who displayed no small curiosity as to who their visitors were and what object they had in coming so far. When they heard that one of the strangers desired to marry the village beauty they shook their heads over him. Did he not know the difficulties in the way? Finding that he would not be turned from his purpose, they led him to a huge rock which overshadowed the village, and described the first test he would be required to meet.

"If you wish to win the maiden," they said, "you must first of all push away that great stone. It is keeping the sunlight from us."

"Alas!" said the youth, "it is impossible."

"Not so," said his companion of the swift foot; "nothing could be more easy."

Saying this, he leaned his shoulder against the rock, and with a mighty crash it fell from its place. From the breaking up of it came the rocks and stones that are scattered all over the world.

The second test was of a different nature. The people brought the strangers a large quantity of food and water, and bade them eat and drink. Being very hungry, they succeeded in disposing of the food, but the suitor sorrowfully regarded the great kettles of water.

"Alas!" said he, "who can drink up that?"

"I can," said the Thirsty One, and in a twinkling he had drunk it all.

The people were amazed at the prowess of the visitors. However, they said, "There is still another test," and they brought out a woman who was a very swift runner, so swift that no one had ever outstripped her in a race.

THE RACE

"You must run a race with this woman," said they. "If you win you shall have the hand of the maiden you have come to seek."

Naturally the suitor chose the Swift One for this test. When the runners were started the people hailed them as fairly matched, for they raced together till they were out of sight.

When they reached the turning point the woman said: "Come, let us rest for a little."

The man agreed, but no sooner had he sat down than he fell asleep. The woman seized her opportunity. Making sure that her rival was sleeping soundly, she set off for the village, running as hard as she could.

Meanwhile the four comrades were anxiously awaiting the return of the competitors, and great was their disappointment when the woman came in sight, while there was yet no sign of their champion.

The man who could hear the plants growing bent his ear to the ground.

"He is asleep," said he; "I can hear him snoring."

The Skilful Archer came forward, and as he bit the point off an arrow he said, "I will soon wake him."

He shot an arrow from the bowstring with such a wonderful aim that it wounded the sleeper's nose, and roused him from his slumbers. The runner started to his feet and looked round for the woman. She was gone. Knowing that he had been tricked, the Swift One put all his energy into an effort to overtake her. She was within a few yards of the winning-post when he passed her. It was a narrow margin, but nevertheless the Swift One had gained the race for his comrade.

The youth was then married to the damsel, whom he found to be all that her admirers had claimed, and more.

THE SNAKE-OGRE

One day a young brave, feeling at variance with the world in general, and wishing to rid himself of the mood, left the lodges of his people and journeyed into the forest. By and by he came to an open space, in the centre of which was a high hill. Thinking he would climb to the top and reconnoitre, he directed his footsteps thither, and as he went he observed a man coming in the opposite direction and making for the same spot. The two met on the summit, and stood for a few moments silently regarding each other. The stranger was the first to speak, gravely inviting the young brave to accompany him to his lodge and sup with him. The other accepted the invitation, and they proceeded in the direction the stranger indicated.

On approaching the lodge the youth saw with some surprise that there was a large heap of bones in front of the door. Within sat a very old woman tending a pot. When the young man learned that the feast was to be a cannibal one, however, he declined to partake of it. The woman thereupon boiled some corn for him, and while doing so told him that his host was nothing more nor less than a snake-man, a sort of ogre who killed and ate human beings. Because the brave was young and very handsome the old woman took pity on him, bemoaning the fate that would surely befall him unless he could escape from the wiles of the snake-man.

"Listen," said she: "I will tell you what to do. Here are some moccasins. When the morning comes put them on your feet, take one step, and you will find yourself on that headland you see in the distance. Give this paper to the man you will meet there, and he will direct you further. But remember that however far you may go, in the evening the Snake will overtake you. When you have finished with the moccasins take them off, place them on the ground facing this way, and they will return."

"Is that all?" said the youth.

"No," she replied. "Before you go you must kill me and put a robe over my bones."

THE MAGIC MOCCASINS

The young brave forthwith proceeded to carry these instructions into effect. First of all he killed the old woman, and disposed of her remains in accordance with her bidding. In the morning he put on the magic moccasins which she had provided for him, and with one great step he reached the distant headland. Here he met an old man, who received the paper from him, and then, giving him another pair of moccasins, directed him to a far-off point where he was to deliver another piece of paper to a man who would await him there. Turning the first moccasins home-ward, the young brave put the second pair to use, and took another gigantic step. Arrived at the second stage of his journey from the Snake's lodge, he found it a repetition of the first. He was directed to another distant spot, and from that to yet another. But when he delivered his message for the fourth time he was treated somewhat differently.

"Down there in the hollow," said the recipient of the paper, "there is a stream. Go toward it, and walk straight on, but do not look at the water."

The youth did as he was bidden, and shortly found himself on the opposite bank of the stream.

He journeyed up the creek, and as evening fell he came upon a place where the river widened to a lake. Skirting its shores, he suddenly found himself face to face with the Snake. Only then did he remember the words of the old woman, who had warned him that in the evening the Snake would overtake him. So he turned himself into a little fish with red fins, lazily moving in the lake.

THE SNAKE'S QUEST

The Snake, high on the bank, saw the little creature, and cried: "Little Fish! have you seen the person I am looking for? If a bird had flown over the lake you must have seen it, the water is so still, and surely you have seen the man I am seeking?"

"Not so," replied the Little Fish, "I have seen no one. But if he passes this way I will tell you."

So the Snake continued downstream, and as he went there was a little grey toad right in his path.

"Little Toad," said he, "have you seen him for whom I am seeking? Even if only a shadow were here you must have seen it."

"Yes," said the Little Toad, "I have seen him, but I cannot tell you which way he has gone."

The Snake doubled and came back on his trail. Seeing a very large fish in shallow water, he said: "Have you seen the man I am looking for?"

"That is he with whom you have just been talking," said the Fish, and the Snake turned homeward. Meeting a muskrat he stopped.

"Have you seen the person I am looking for?" he said. Then, having his suspicions aroused, he added craftily: "I think that you are he."

But the Muskrat began a bitter complaint.

"Just now," said he, "the person you seek passed over my lodge and broke it."

So the Snake passed on, and encountered a red-breasted turtle.

He repeated his query, and the Turtle told him that the object of his search was to be met with farther on.

"But beware," he added, "for if you do not recognize him he will kill you."

Following the stream, the Snake came upon a large green frog floating in shallow water.

"I have been seeking a person since morning," he said. "I think that you are he."

The Frog allayed his suspicions, saying: "You will meet him farther down the stream."

The Snake next found a large turtle floating among the green scum on a lake. Getting the Turtle's back, he said: "You must be the person I seek," and his head rose higher and higher as he prepared to strike.

"I am not," replied the Turtle. "The next person you meet will be he. But beware, for if you do not recognize him he will kill you."

When he had gone a little farther down the Snake attempted to cross the stream. In the middle was an eddy. Crafty as he was, the Snake failed to recognize his enemy, and the eddy drew him down into the water and drowned him. So the youth succeeded in slaying the Snake who had sought throughout the day to kill him.

THE STORY OF THE SALMON

A certain chief who had a very beautiful daughter was unwilling to part with her, but knowing that the time must come when she would marry he arranged a contest for her suitors, in which the feat was to break a pair of elk's antlers hung in the centre of the lodge.

"Whoever shall break these antlers," the old chief declared, "shall have the hand of my daughter."

The quadrupeds came first—the Snail, Squirrel, Otter, Beaver, Wolf, Bear, and Panther; but all their strength and skill would not suffice to break the antlers. Next came the Birds, but their efforts also were unavailing. The only creature left who had not attempted the feat was a feeble thing covered with sores, whom the mischievous Blue Jay derisively summoned to perform the task. After repeated taunts from the tricky bird, the creature rose, shook itself, and became whole and clean and very good to look upon, and the assembled company saw that it was the Salmon. He grasped the elk's antlers and easily broke them in five pieces. Then, claiming his prize, the chief's daughter, he led her away.

Before they had gone very far the people said: "Let us go and take the chief's daughter back," and they set off in pursuit of the pair along the seashore.

When Salmon saw what was happening he created a bay between himself and his pursuers. The people at length reached the point of the bay on which Salmon stood, but he made another bay, and when they looked they could see him on the far-off point of that one. So the chase went on, till Salmon grew tired of exercising his magic powers.

Coyote and Badger, who were in advance of the others, decided to shoot at Salmon. The arrow hit him in the neck and killed him instantly. When the rest of the band came up they gave the chief's daughter to the Wolves, and she became the wife of one of them.

In due time the people returned to their village, and the Crow, who was Salmon's aunt, learnt of his death. She hastened away to the spot where he had been killed, to seek his remains, but all she could find was one salmon's egg, which she hid in a hole in the riverbank. Next day she found that the egg was much larger, on the third day it was a small trout, and so it grew till it became a full-grown salmon, and at length a handsome youth.

SALMON'S MAGIC BATH

Leading young Salmon to a mountain pool, his grand-aunt said: "Bathe there, that you may see spirits."

One day Salmon said: "I am tired of seeing spirits. Let me go away."

The old Crow thereupon told him of his father's death at the hands of Badger and Coyote.

"They have taken your father's bow," she said.

The Salmon shot an arrow toward the forest, and the forest went on fire. He shot an arrow toward the prairie, and it also caught fire.

"Truly," muttered the old Crow, "you have seen spirits."

Having made up his mind to get his father's bow, Salmon journeyed to the lodge where Coyote and Badger dwelt. He found the door shut, and the creatures with their faces blackened, pretending to lament the death of old Salmon. However, he was not deceived by their tricks, but boldly entered and demanded his father's bow. Four times they gave him other bows, which broke when he drew them. The fifth time it was really his father's bow he received. Taking Coyote and Badger outside, he knocked them together and killed them.

THE WOLF LODGE

As he travelled across the prairie he stumbled on the habitation of the Wolves, and on entering the lodge he encountered his father's wife, who bade him hide before the monsters returned. By means of strategy he got the better of them, shot them all, and sailed away in a little boat with the woman. Here he fell into a deep sleep, and slept so long that at last his companion ventured to wake him. Very angry at being roused, he turned her into a pigeon and cast her out of the boat, while he himself, as a salmon, swam to the shore.

Near the edge of the water was a lodge, where dwelt five beautiful sisters. Salmon sat on the shore at a little distance, and took the form of an aged man covered with sores. When the eldest sister came down to speak to him he bade her carry him on her back to the lodge, but so loathsome a creature was he that she beat a hasty retreat. The second sister did likewise, and the third, and the fourth. But the youngest sister proceeded to carry him to the lodge, where he became again a young and handsome brave. He married all the sisters, but the youngest was his head-wife and his favourite.

THE DROWNED CHILD

On the banks of a river there dwelt a worthy couple with their only son, a little child whom they loved dearly. One day the boy wandered away from the lodge and fell into the water, and no one was near enough to rescue him. Great was the distress of the parents when the news reached them, and all his kindred were loud in their lamentations, for the child had been a favourite with everybody. The father especially showed signs of the deepest grief, and refused to enter his lodge till he should recover the boy. All night he lay outside on the bare ground, his cheek pillowed on his hand. Suddenly he heard a faint sound, far under the earth. He listened intently: it was the crying of his lost child! Hastily he gathered all his relatives round him, told them what he had heard, and besought them piteously to dig into the earth and bring back his son. This task they hesitated to undertake, but they willingly collected horses and goods in abundance, to be given to anyone who would venture.

Two men came forward who claimed to possess supernatural powers, and to them was entrusted the work of finding the child. The grateful father gave them a pipe filled with tobacco, and promised them all his possessions if their mission should succeed. The two gifted men painted their bodies, one making himself quite black, the other yellow. Going to the neighbouring river, they plunged into its depths, and so arrived at the abode of the Water-god. This being and his wife, having no children of their own, had adopted the Indian's little son who was supposed to have been drowned, and the two men, seeing him alive and well, were pleased to think that their task was as good as accomplished.

"The father has sent for his son," they said. "He has commanded us to bring him back. We dare not return without him."

"You are too late," responded the Water-god. "Had you come before he had eaten my food he might safely have returned with you. But he wished to eat, and he has eaten, and now, alas! he would die if he were taken out of the water."[1]

Sorrowfully the men rose to the surface and carried the tidings to the father.

"Alas!" they said, "he has eaten in the palace of the Water-god. He will die if we bring him home."

Nevertheless the father persisted in his desire to see the child.

"I must see him," he said, and the two men prepared for a second journey, saying: "If you get him back, the Water-god will require a white dog in payment."

The Indian promised to supply the dog. The two men painted themselves again, the one black, the other yellow. Once more they dived through the limpid water to the palace of the god.

"The father must have his child," they said. "This time we dare not return without him."

So the deity gave up the little boy, who was placed in his father's arms, dead. At the sight the grief of his kindred burst out afresh. However, they did not omit to cast a white dog into the river, nor to pay the men lavishly, as they had promised.

Later the parents lost a daughter in the same manner, but as she had eaten nothing of the food offered to her under the water she was brought back alive, on payment by her relatives of a tribute to the Water-god of four white-haired dogs.

THE SNAKE-WIFE

A certain chief advised his son to travel. Idling, he pointed out, was not the way to qualify for chieftainship.

"When I was your age," said he, "I did not sit still. There was hard work to be done. And now look at me: I have become a great chief."

"I will go hunting, father," said the youth. So his father furnished him with good clothing, and had a horse saddled for him.

The young man went off on his expedition, and by and by fell in with some elk. Shooting at the largest beast, he wounded it but slightly, and as it dashed away he spurred his horse after it. In this manner they covered a considerable distance, till at length the hunter, worn-out with thirst and fatigue, reined in his steed and dismounted. He wandered about in search of water till he was well-nigh spent, but after a time he came upon a spring, and immediately improvised a song of thanks-giving to the deity, Wakanda, who had permitted him to find it. His rejoicing was somewhat premature, however, for when he approached the spring a snake started up from it. The youth was badly scared, and retreated to a safe distance without drinking. It seemed as though he must die of thirst after all. Venturing to look back after a time, he saw that the snake had disappeared, and very cautiously he returned. Again the snake darted from the water, and the thirsty hunter was forced to flee. A third return to the spring had no happier results, but when his thirst drove him to a fourth attempt the youth found, instead of a snake, a very beautiful woman. She offered him a drink in a small cup, which she replenished as often as he emptied it. So struck was he by her grace and beauty that he promptly fell in love with her. When it was time for him to return home she gave him a ring, saying: "When you sit down to eat, place this ring on a seat and say, 'Come, let us eat,' and I will come to you."

Having bidden her farewell, the young man turned his steps home-ward, and when he was once more among his kindred and asked that food might be placed before him. "Make haste," said he, "for I am very hungry."

Quickly they obeyed him, and set down a variety of dishes. When he was alone the youth drew the ring from his finger and laid it on a seat. "Come," he said, "let us eat."

Immediately the Snake-woman appeared and joined him at his meal. When she had eaten she vanished as mysteriously as she had come, and the disconsolate husband (for the youth had married her) went out of the lodge to seek her. Thinking she might be among the women of the village, he said to his father: "Let the women dance before me."

An old man was deputed to gather the women together, but not one of them so much as resembled the Snake-woman.

Again the youth sat down to eat, and repeated the formula which his wife had described to him. She ate with him as before, and vanished when the meal was over.

"Father," said the young man, "let the very young women dance before me."

But the Snake-woman was not found among them either.

Another fleeting visit from his wife induced the chief's son to make yet another attempt to find her in the community.

"Let the young girls dance," he said. Still the mysterious Snake-woman was not found.

One day a girl overheard voices in the youth's lodge, and, peering in, saw a beautiful woman sharing his meal. She told the news to the chief, and it soon became known that the chief's son was married to a beautiful stranger.

The youth, however, wished to marry a woman of his own tribe; but the maiden's father, having heard that the young man was already married, told his daughter that she was only being made fun of.

So the girl had nothing more to do with her wooer, who turned for consolation to his ring. He caused food to be brought, and placed the ring on a seat.

THE RING UNAVAILING

"Come," he said, "let us eat."

There was no response; the Snake-woman would not appear.

The youth was greatly disappointed, and made up his mind to go in search of his wife.

"I am going a–hunting," said he, and again his father gave him good clothes and saddled a horse for him.

When he reached the spot where the Snake-woman had first met him, he found her trail leading up to the spring, and beyond it on the other side. Still following the trail, he saw before him a very dilapidated lodge, at the door of which sat an old man in rags. The youth felt very sorry for the tattered fellow, and gave him his fine clothes, in exchange for which he received the other's rags.

"You think you are doing me a good turn," said the old man, "but it is I who am going to do you one. The woman you seek has gone over the Great Water. When you get to the other shore talk with the people you shall meet there, and if they do not obey you send them away."

In addition to the tattered garments, the old man gave him a hat, a sword, and a lame old horse.

At the edge of the Great Water the youth prepared to cross, while his companion seated himself on the shore, closed his eyes, and recited a spell. In a moment the young man found himself on the opposite shore. Here he found a lodge inhabited by two aged Thunder-men, who were apparently given to eating human beings. The young stranger made the discovery that his hat rendered him invisible, and he was able to move unseen among the creatures. Taking off his hat for a moment, he took the pipe from the lips of a Thunder-man and pressed it against the latter's hand.

"Oh," cried the Thunder-man, "I am burnt!"

But the youth had clapped on his hat and disappeared.

"It is not well," said the Thunder-man gravely. "A stranger has been here and we have let him escape. When our brother returns he will not believe us if we tell him the man has vanished."

Shortly after this another Thunder-man entered with the body of a man he had killed. When the brothers told him their story he was quite sceptical.

"If I had been here," said he, "I would not have let him escape."

As he spoke the youth snatched his pipe from him and pressed it against the back of his hand.

"Oh," said the Thunder-man, "I am burnt!"

"It was not I," said one brother.

"It was not I," said the other.

"It was I," said the youth, pulling off his hat and appearing among them. "What were you talking about among yourselves? Here I am. Do as you said."

But the Thunder-men were afraid.

"We were not speaking," they said, and the youth put on his hat and vanished.

"What will our brother say," cried the three in dismay, "when he hears that a man has been here and we have not killed him? Our brother will surely hate us."

In a few minutes another Thunder-man came into the lodge, carrying the body of a child. He was very angry when he heard that they had let a man escape.

The youth repeated his trick on the newcomer—appeared for a moment, then vanished again. The fifth and last of the brothers was also deceived in the same manner.

Seeing that the monsters were now thoroughly frightened, the young man took off his magic hat and talked with them.

THE FINDING OF THE SNAKE-WIFE

"You do wrong," said he, "to eat men like this. You should eat buffaloes, not men. I am going away. When I come back I will visit you, and if you are eating buffaloes you shall remain, but if you are eating men I shall send you away."

The Thunder-men promised they would eat only buffaloes in the future, and the young man went on his way to seek for the Snake-woman. When at last he came to the village where she dwelt he found she had married a man of another tribe, and in a great rage he swung the sword the magician had given him and slew her, and her husband, and the whole village, after which he returned the way he had come. When he reached the lodge of the Thunder-men he saw that they had not kept their promise to eat only buffaloes.

"I am going to send you above," he said. "Hitherto you have destroyed men, but when I have sent you away you shall give them cooling rain to keep them alive."

So he sent them above, where they became the thunder-clouds.

Proceeding on his journey, he again crossed the Great Water with a single stride, and related to the old wizard all that had happened.

"I have sent the Thunder-men above, because they would not stop eating men. Have I done well?"

"Very well.

"I have killed the whole village where the Snake-woman was, because she had taken another husband. Have I done well?"

"Very well. It was for that I gave you the sword."

The youth returned to his father, and married a very beautiful woman of his own village.

A SUBTERRANEAN ADVENTURE

There lived in a populous village a chief who had two sons and one daughter, all of them unmarried. Both the sons were in the habit of joining the hunters when they went to shoot buffaloes, and on one such occasion a large animal became separated from the herd. One of the chief's sons followed it, and when the pursuit had taken him some distance from the rest of the party the buffalo suddenly disappeared into a large pit. Before they could check themselves man and horse had plunged in after him. When the hunters returned the chief was greatly disturbed to learn that his son was missing. He sent the criers in all directions, and spared no pains to get news of the youth.

"If any person knows the whereabouts of the chief's son," shouted the criers, "let him come and tell."

This they repeated again and again, till at length a young man came forward who had witnessed the accident.

"I was standing on a hill," he said, "and I saw the hunters, and I saw the son of the chief. And when he was on level ground he disappeared, and I saw him no more."

He led the men of the tribe to the spot, and they scattered to look for signs of the youth. They found his trail; they followed it to the pit, and there it stopped.

They pitched their tents round the chasm, and the chief begged his people to descend into it to search for his son.

"If any man among you is brave and stout-hearted," he said, "let him enter."

There was no response.

"If anyone will go I will make him rich."

Still no one ventured to speak.

"If anyone will go I will give him my daughter in marriage."

There was a stir among the braves and a youth came forward.

"I will go," he said simply.

Ropes of hide were made by willing hands, and secured to a skin shaped to form a sort of bucket.

After arranging signals with the party at the mouth of the pit, the adventurous searcher allowed himself to be lowered. Once fairly launched in the Cimmerian depths his eyes became accustomed to the darkness, and he saw first the buffalo, then the horse, then the young brave, quite dead. He put the body of the chief's son into the skin bucket, and gave the signal for it to be drawn up to the surface. But so great was the excitement that when his comrades had drawn up the dead man they forgot about the living one still in the pit, and hurried away.

LOST UNDERGROUND

By and by the hero got tired of shouting, and wandered off into the darkness.

He had not gone very far when he met an old woman. Respectfully addressing her, he told her his story and begged her to aid his return to his own country.

"Indeed I cannot help you," she said, "but if you will go to the house of the wise man who lives round the corner you may get what you want."

Having followed the direction she had indicated with a withered finger, the youth shortly arrived at a lodge. Hungry and weary, he knocked somewhat impatiently. Receiving no answer, he knocked again, still more loudly. This time there was a movement inside the lodge, and a woman came to the door. She led him inside, where her husband sat dejectedly, not even rising to greet the visitor. Sadly the woman told him that they were mourning the death of their only son. At a word from his wife the husband looked at the youth. Eagerly he rose and embraced him.

"You are like our lost child," said he. "Come and we will make you our son."

The young brave then told him his story.

"We shall treat you as our child," said the Wise Man. "Whatever you shall ask we will give you, even should you desire to leave us and to return to your own people."

Though he was touched by the kindness of the good folk, there was yet nothing the youth desired so much as to return to his kindred.

"Give me," said he, "a white horse and a white mule."

THE RETURN TO EARTH

The old man bade him go to where the horses were hobbled, and there he found what he had asked for. He also received from his host a magic piece of iron, which would enable him to obtain whatever he desired.

The rocks even melted away at a touch of this talisman. Thus equipped, the adventurer rode off.

Shortly afterward he emerged in his own country, where the first persons he met were the chief and his wife, to whom he disclosed his identity, as he was by this time very much changed. They were sceptical at first, but soon they came to recognize him, and gave him a very cordial reception.

He married the chief's daughter, and was made head chieftain by his father-in-law. The people built a lodge for him in the centre of the encampment, and brought him many valuable presents of clothing and horses. On his marriage-day the criers were sent out to tell the people that on the following day no one must leave the village or do any work.

On the morrow all the men of the tribe went out to hunt buffaloes, and the young chieftain accompanied them. By means of his magic piece of iron he charmed many buffaloes, and slew more than did the others.

Now it so happened that the chief's remaining son was very jealous of his brother-in-law. He thought his father should have given him the chieftainship, and the honours accorded by the people to his young relative were exceedingly galling to him. So he made up his mind to kill the youth and destroy his beautiful white horse. But the sagacious beast told its master that someone was plotting against his life, and, duly warned, he watched in the stable every night.

On the occasion of a second great buffalo hunt the wicked schemer found his opportunity. By waving his robe he scared the buffaloes and caused them to close in on the youth and trample him to death. But when the herd had scattered and moved away there was no trace of the young brave or of his milk-white steed. They had returned to the Underworld.

WHITE FEATHER THE GIANT-KILLER

There once dwelt in the heart of a great forest an old man and his grandchild. So far as he could remember, the boy had never seen any human being but his grandfather, and though he frequently questioned the latter on the subject of his relatives he could elicit no information from him. The truth was that they had perished at the hands of six great giants. The nation to which the boy belonged had wagered their children against those of the giants that they would beat the latter in a race. Unfortunately the giants won, the children of the rash Indians were forfeited, and all were slain with the exception of little Chácopee, whose grandfather had taken charge of him. The child learned to hunt and fish, and seemed quite contented and happy.

One day the boy wandered away to the edge of a prairie, where he found traces of an encampment. Returning, he told his grandfather of the ashes and tent-poles he had seen, and asked for an explanation. Had his grandfather set them there? The old man responded brusquely that there were no ashes or tent-poles: he had merely imagined them. The boy was sorely puzzled, but he let the matter drop, and next day he followed a different path. Quite suddenly he heard a voice addressing him as "Wearer of the White Feather." Now there had been a tradition in his tribe that a mighty man would arise among them wearing a white feather and performing prodigies of valour. But of this Chácopee as yet knew nothing, so he could only look about him in a startled way. Close by him stood a man, which fact was in itself sufficiently astonishing to the boy, who had never seen anyone but his grandfather; but to his further bewilderment he perceived that the man was made of wood from the breast downward, only the head being of flesh.

"You do not wear the white feather yet," the curious stranger resumed, "but you will by and by. Go home and sleep. You will dream of a pipe, a sack, and a large white feather. When you wake you will see these things by your side. Put the feather on your head and you will become a very great warrior. If you want proof, smoke the pipe and you will see the smoke turn into pigeons."

He then proceeded to tell him who his parents were, and of the manner in which they had perished, and bade him avenge their death on the giants. To aid him in the accomplishment of this feat he gave him a magic vine which would be invisible to the giants, and with which he must trip them up when they ran a race with him.

Chácopee returned home, and everything happened as the Man of Wood had predicted. The old grandfather was greatly surprised to see a flock of pigeons issuing from the lodge, from which Chácopee also shortly emerged, wearing on his head a white feather. Remembering the prophecy, the old man wept to think that he might lose his grandchild.

IN SEARCH OF THE GIANTS

Next morning Chácopee set off in search of the giants, whom he found in a very large lodge in the centre of the forest. The giants had learned of his approach from the "little spirits who carry the news." Among themselves they mocked and scoffed at him, but outwardly they greeted him with much civility, which, however, in nowise deceived him as to their true feelings. Without loss of time they arranged a race between Chácopee and the youngest giant, the winner of which was to cut off the head of the other. Chácopee won, with the help of his magic vine, and killed his opponent. Next morning he appeared again, and decapitated another of his foes. This happened on five mornings. On the sixth he set out as usual, but was met by the Man of Wood, who informed him that on his way to the giants' lodge he would encounter the most beautiful woman in the world.

CHÁCOPEE'S DOWNFALL

"Pay no attention to her," he said earnestly. "She is there for your destruction. When you see her turn yourself into an elk, and you will be safe from her wiles."

Chácopee proceeded on his way, and sure enough before long he met the most beautiful woman in the world. Mindful of the advice he had received, he turned himself into an elk, but, instead of passing by, the woman, who was really the sixth giant, came up to him and reproached him with tears for taking the form of an elk when she had travelled so far to become his wife. Chácopee was so touched by her grief and beauty that he resumed his own shape and endeavoured to console her with gentle words and caresses. At last he fell asleep with his head in her lap. The beautiful woman once more became the cruel giant, and, seizing his axe, the monster broke Chácopee's back; then, turning him into a dog, he bade him rise and follow him. The white feather he stuck in his own head, fancying that magic powers accompanied the wearing of it.

In the path of the travellers there lay a certain village in which dwelt two young girls, the daughters of a chief. Having heard the prophecy concerning the wearer of the white feather, each made up her mind that she would marry him when he should appear. Therefore, when they saw a man approaching with a white feather in his hair the elder ran to meet him, invited him into her lodge, and soon after married him. The younger, who was gentle and timid, took the dog into her home and treated him with great kindness.

One day while the giant was out hunting he saw the dog casting a stone into the water. Immediately the stone became a beaver, which the dog caught and killed. The giant strove to emulate this feat, and was successful, but when he went home and ordered his wife to go outside and fetch the beaver only a stone lay by the door. Next day he saw the dog plucking a withered branch and throwing it on the ground, where it became a deer, which the dog slew. The giant performed this magic feat also, but when his wife went to the door of the lodge to fetch the deer she saw only a piece of rotten wood. Nevertheless the giant had some success in the chase, and his wife repaired to the home of her father to tell him what a skilful hunter her husband was. She also spoke of the dog that lived with her sister, and his skill in the chase.

THE TRANSFORMATION

The old chief suspected magic, and sent a deputation of youths and maidens to invite his younger daughter and her dog to visit him. To the surprise of the deputation, no dog was there, but an exceedingly handsome warrior. But alas! Chácopee could not speak. The party set off for the home of the old chief, where they were warmly welcomed.

It was arranged to hold a general meeting, so that the wearer of the white feather might show his prowess and magical powers. First of all they took the giant's pipe (which had belonged to Chácopee), and the warriors smoked it one after the other. When it came to Chácopee's turn he signified that the giant should precede him. The giant smoked, but to the disappointment of the assembly nothing unusual happened. Then Chácopee took the pipe, and as the smoke ascended it became a flock of pigeons. At the same moment he recovered his speech, and recounted his strange adventures to the astounded listeners. Their indignation against the giant was unbounded, and the chief ordered that he should be given the form of a dog and stoned to death by the people.

Chácopee gave a further proof of his right to wear the white feather. Calling for a buffalo-hide, he cut it into little pieces and strewed it on the prairie. Next day he summoned the braves of the tribe to a buffalo-hunt, and at no great distance they found a magnificent herd. The pieces of hide had become buffaloes. The people greeted this exhibition of magic art with loud acclamations, and Chácopee's reputation was firmly established with the tribe.

Chácopee begged the chief's permission to take his wife on a visit to his grandfather, which was readily granted, and the old man's gratitude and delight more than repaid them for the perils of their journey.

HOW THE RABBIT CAUGHT THE SUN

Once upon a time the Rabbit dwelt in a lodge with no one but his grandmother to keep him company. Every morning he went hunting very early, but no matter how early he was he always noticed that someone with a very long foot had been before him and had left a trail. The Rabbit resolved to discover the identity of the hunter who forestalled him, so one fine morning he rose even earlier than usual, in the hope of encountering the stranger. But all to no purpose, for the mysterious one had gone, leaving behind him, as was his wont, the trail of the long foot.

This irritated the Rabbit profoundly, and he returned to the lodge to consult with his grandmother.

"Grandmother," he grumbled, "although I rise early every morning and set my traps in the hope of snaring game, someone is always before me and frightens the game away. I shall make a snare and catch him."

"Why should you do so?" replied his grandmother. "In what way has he harmed you?"

"It is sufficient that I hate him," replied the querulous Rabbit, and departed. He secreted himself among the bushes and waited for nightfall. He had provided himself with a stout bowstring, which he arranged as a trap in the place where the footprints were usually to be found. Then he went home, but returned very early to examine his snare.

When he arrived at the spot he discovered that he had caught the intruder, who was, indeed, no less a personage than the Sun. He ran home at the top of his speed to acquaint his grandmother with the news. He did not know what he had caught, so his grandmother bade him seek the forest once more and find out. On returning he saw that the Sun was in a violent passion.

"How dare you snare me!" he cried angrily. "Come hither and untie me at once!"

The Rabbit advanced cautiously, and circled round him in abject terror. At last he ducked his head and, running in, cut the bowstring which secured the Sun with his knife. The Sun immediately soared upward, and was quickly lost to sight. And the reason why the hair between the Rabbit's shoulders is yellow is that he was scorched there by the great heat which came from the Sun-god when he loosed him.

HOW THE RABBIT SLEW THE DEVOURING HILL

In the long ago there existed a hill of ogre-like propensities which drew people into its mouth and devoured them. The Rabbit's grandmother warned him not to approach it upon any account.

But the Rabbit was rash, and the very fact that he had been warned against the vicinity made him all the more anxious to visit it. So he went to the hill, and cried mockingly: "Pahe-Wathahuni, draw me into your mouth! Come, devour me!"

But Pahe-Wathahuni knew the Rabbit, so he took no notice of him.

Shortly afterward a hunting-party came that way, and Pahe-Wathahuni opened his mouth, so that they took it to be a great cavern, and entered. The Rabbit, waiting his chance, pressed in behind them. But when he reached Pahe-Wathahuni's stomach the monster felt that something disagreed with him, and he vomited up the Rabbit.

Later in the day another hunting-party appeared, and Pahe-Wathahuni again opened his capacious gullet. The hunters entered unwittingly, and were devoured. And once more the Rabbit entered, disguised as a man by magic art. This time the cannibal hill did not eject him. Imprisoned in the monster's entrails, he saw in the distance the whitened bones of folk who had been devoured, the still undigested bodies of others, and some who were yet alive.

Mocking Pahe-Wathahuni, the Rabbit said: "Why do you not eat? You should have eaten that very fat heart." And, seizing his knife, he made as if to devour it. At this Pahe-Wathahuni set up a dismal howling; but the Rabbit merely mocked him, and slit the heart in twain. At this the hill split asunder, and all the folk who had been imprisoned within it went out again, stretched their arms to the blue sky, and hailed the Rabbit as their deliverer; for it was Pahe-Wathahuni's heart that had been sundered.

The people gathered together and said: "Let us make the Rabbit chief." But he mocked them and told them to be gone, that all he desired was the heap of fat the hill had concealed within its entrails, which would serve him and his old grandmother for food for many a day. With that the Rabbit went homeward, carrying the fat on his back, and he and his grandmother rejoiced exceedingly and were never in want again.

IV

MYTHS AND LEGENDS
OF THE PAWNEES

THE PAWNEES, OR CADDOAN INDIANS

THE CADDOAN stock, the principal representatives of which are the Pawnees, are now settled in Oklahoma and North Dakota. From the earliest period they seem to have been cultivators of the soil, as well as hunters, and skilled in the arts of weaving and pottery-making. They possessed an elaborate form of religious ceremonial. The following myths well exemplify how strongly the Pawnee was gifted with the religious sense.

THE SACRED BUNDLE

A certain young man was very vain of his personal appearance, and always wore the finest clothes and richest adornments he could procure. Among other possessions he had a down feather of an eagle, which he wore on his head when he went to war, and which possessed magical properties. He was unmarried, and care nothing for women, though doubtless there was more than one maiden of the village who would not have disdained the hand of the young hunter, for he was as brave and good-natured as he was handsome.

One day while he was out hunting with his companions—the Indians hunted on foot in those days—he got separated from the others, and followed some buffaloes for a considerable distance. The animals managed to escape, with the exception of a young cow, which had become stranded in a mud-hole. The youth fitted an arrow to his bow, and was about to fire, when he saw that the buffalo had vanished and only a young and pretty woman was in sight. The hunter was rather perplexed, for he could not understand where the animal had gone to, nor where the woman had come from. However, he talked to the maiden, and found her so agreeable that he proposed to marry her and return with her to his tribe. She consented to marry him, but only on condition that they remained where they were. To this he agreed, and gave her as a wedding gift a string of blue and white beads he wore round his neck.

One evening when he returned home after a day's hunting he found that his camp was gone, and all round about were the marks of many hoofs. No trace of his wife's body could he discover, and at last, mourning her bitterly, he returned to his tribe.

Years elapsed, and one summer morning as he was playing the stick game with his friends a little boy came toward him, wearing round his neck a string of blue and white beads.

"Father," he said, "mother wants you."

The hunter was annoyed at the interruption.

"I am not your father," he replied. "Go away."

The boy went away, and the man's companions laughed at him when they heard him addressed as "father," for they knew he was a woman-hater and unmarried.

However, the boy returned in a little while. He was sent away again by the angry hunter, but one of the players now suggested that he should accompany the child and see what he wanted. All the time the hunter had been wondering where he had seen the beads before. As he reflected he saw a buffalo cow and calf running across the prairie, and suddenly he remembered.

Taking his bow and arrows, he followed the buffaloes, whom he now recognized as his wife and child. A long and wearisome journey they had. The woman was angry with her husband, and dried up every creek they came to, so that he feared he would die of thirst, but the strategy of his son obtained food and drink for him until they arrived at the home of the buffaloes. The big bulls, the leaders of the herd, were very angry, and threatened to kill him. First, however, they gave him a test, telling him that if he accomplished it he should live. Six cows, all exactly alike, were placed in a row, and he was told that if he could point out his wife his life would be spared. His son helped him secretly, and he succeeded. The old bulls were surprised, and much annoyed, for they had not expected him to distinguish his wife from the other cows. They gave him another test. He was requested to pick out his son from among several calves. Again the young buffalo helped him to perform the feat. Not yet satisfied, they decreed that he must run a race. If he should win they would let him go. They chose their fastest runners, but on the day set for the race a thin coating of ice covered the ground, and the buffaloes could not run at all, while the young Indian ran swiftly and steadily, and won with ease.

THE MAGIC FEATHER

The chief bulls were still angry, however, and determined that they would kill him, even though he had passed their tests. So they made him sit on the ground, all the strongest and fiercest bulls round him. Together they rushed at him, and in a little while his feather was seen floating in the air.

The chief bulls called on the others to stop, for they were sure that he must be trampled to pieces by this time. But when they drew back there sat the Indian in the centre of the circle, with his feather in his hair.

It was, in fact, his magic feather to which he owed his escape, and a second rush which the buffaloes made had as little effect on him. Seeing that he was possessed of magical powers, the buffaloes made the best of matters and welcomed him into their camp, on the condition that he would bring them gifts from his tribe. This he agreed to do.

When the Indian returned with his wife and son to the village people they found that there was no food to be had; but the buffalo-wife produced some meat from under her robe, and they ate it. Afterward they went back to the herd with gifts, which pleased the buffaloes greatly. The chief bulls, knowing that the people were in want of food, offered to return with the hunter. His son, who also wished to return, arranged to accompany the herd in the form of a buffalo, while his parents went ahead in human shape. The father warned the people that they must not kill his son when they went to hunt buffaloes, for, he said, the yellow calf would always return leading more buffaloes.

By and by the child came to his father saying that he would no more visit the camp in the form of a boy, as he was about to lead the herd eastward. Ere he went he told his father that when the hunters sought the chase they should kill the yellow calf and sacrifice it to Atíus Tiráwa, tan its hide, and wrap in the skin an ear of corn and other sacred things. Every year they should look out for another yellow calf, sacrifice it, and keep a piece of its fat to add to the bundle. Then when food was scarce and famine threatened the tribe the chiefs should gather in council and pay a friendly visit to the young buffalo, and he would tell Tiráwa of their need, so that another yellow calf might be sent to lead the herd to the people.

When he had said this the boy left the camp. All was done as he had ordered. Food became plentiful, and the father became a chief, greatly respected by his people. His buffalo-wife, however, he almost forgot, and one night she vanished. So distressed was the chief, and so remorseful for his neglect of her, that he never recovered, but withered away and died. But the sacred bundle was long preserved in the tribe as a magic charm to bring the buffalo.

Their sacred bundles were most precious to the Indians, and were guarded religiously. In times of famine they were opened by the priests with much ceremony. The above story is given to explain the origin of that belonging to the Pawnee tribe.

THE BEAR-MAN

There was once a boy of the Pawnee tribe who imitated the ways of a bear; and, indeed, he much resembled that animal. When he played with the other boys of his village he would pretend to be a bear, and even when he grew up he would often tell his companions laughingly that he could turn himself into a bear whenever he liked.

His resemblance to the animal came about in this manner. Before the boy was born his father had gone on the warpath, and at some distance from his home had come upon a tiny bear-cub. The little creature looked at him so wistfully and was so small and helpless that he could not pass by without taking notice of it. So he stooped and picked it up in his arms, tied some Indian tobacco round its neck, and said: "I know that the Great Spirit, Tiráwa, will care for you, but I cannot go on my way without putting these things round your neck to show that I feel kindly toward you. I hope that the animals will take care of my son when he is born, and help him to grow up a great and wise man." With that he went on his way.

On his return he told his wife of his encounter with the Little Bear, told her how he had taken it in his arms and looked at it and talked to it. Now there is an Indian superstition that a woman, before a child is born, must not look fixedly at or think much about any animal, or the infant will resemble it. So when the warrior's boy was born he was found to have the ways of a bear, and to become more and more like that animal the older he grew. The boy, quite aware of the resemblance, often went away by himself into the forest, where he used to pray to the Bear.

THE BEAR-MAN SLAIN

On one occasion, when he was quite grown up, he accompanied a war-party of the Pawnees as their chief. They travelled a considerable distance, but ere they arrived at any village they fell into a trap prepared for them by their enemies, the Sioux. Taken completely off their guard, the Pawnees, to the number of about forty, were slain to a man. The part of the country in which this incident took place was rocky and cedar-clad and harboured many bears, and the bodies of the dead Pawnees lay in a ravine in the path of these animals. When they came to the body of the Bear-man a she-bear instantly recognized it as that of their benefactor, who had sacrificed smokes to them, made songs about them, and done them many a good turn during his lifetime. She called to her companion and begged him to do something to bring the Bear-man to life again. The other protested that he could do nothing. "Nevertheless," he added, "I will try. If the sun were shining I might succeed, but when it is dark and cloudy I am powerless."

THE RESUSCITATION OF THE BEAR-MAN

The sun was shining but fitfully that day, however. Long intervals of gloom succeeded each gleam of sunlight. But the two bears set about collecting the remains of the Bear-man, who was indeed sadly mutilated, and, lying down on his body, they worked over him with their magic medicine till he showed signs of returning life. At length he fully regained consciousness, and, finding himself in the presence of two bears, was at a loss to know what had happened to him. But the animals related how they had brought him to life, and the sight of his dead comrades lying around him recalled what had gone before. Gratefully acknowledging the service the bears had done him, he accompanied them to their den. he was still very weak, and frequently fainted, but ere long he recovered his strength and was as well as ever, only he had no hair on his head, for the Sioux had scalped him. During his sojourn with the bears he was taught all the things that they knew—which was a great deal, for all Indians know that the bear is one of the wisest animals. However, his host begged him not to regard the wonderful things he did as the outcome of his own strength, but to give thanks to Tiráwa, who had made the bears and had given them their wisdom and greatness. Finally he told the Bear-man to return to his people, where he would become a very great man, great in war and in wealth. But at the same time he must not forget the bears, nor cease to imitate them, for on that would depend much of his success.

"I shall look after you," he concluded. "If I die, you shall die; if I grow old, you shall grow old along with me. This tree"—pointing to a cedar—"shall be a protector to you. It never becomes old; it is always fresh and beautiful, the gift of Tiráwa. And if a thunderstorm should come while you are at home throw some cedarwood on the fire and you will be safe."

Giving him a bearskin cap to hide his hairless scalp, the bears then bade him depart.

Arrived at his home, the young man was greeted with amazement, for it was thought that he had perished with the rest of the war-party. But when he convinced his parents that it was indeed their son who visited them, they received him joyfully. When he had embraced his friends and had been congratulated by them on his return, he told them of the bears, who were waiting outside the village. Taking presents of Indian tobacco, sweet-smelling clay, buffalo-meat, and beads, he returned to them, and again talked with the he-bear. The latter hugged him, saying: "As my fur has touched you, you will be great; as my hands have touched your hands, you will be fearless; and as my mouth has touched your mouth, you will be wise." With that the bears departed.

True to his words, the animal made the Bear-man the greatest warrior of his tribe. He was the originator of the Bear Dance, which the Pawnees still practice. He lived to an advanced age, greatly honoured by his people.

V

MYTHS AND LEGENDS OF THE NORTHERN AND NORTHWESTERN INDIANS

HAIDA DEMIGODS

THERE IS a curious Haida story told of the origin of certain supernatural people, who are supposed to speak through the *shamans,* or medicine-men, and of how they got their names.

Ten brothers went out to hunt with their dogs. While they were climbing a steep rocky mountain a thick mist enveloped them, and they were compelled to remain on the heights. By and by they made a fire, and the youngest, who was full of mischief, cast his bow in it. When the bow was burnt the hunters were astonished to see it on the level ground below. The mischievous brother thereupon announced his intention of following his weapon, and by the same means. Though the others tried hard to dissuade him, he threw himself on the blazing fire, and was quickly consumed. His brothers then beheld him on the plain vigorously exhorting them to follow his example. One by one they did so, some boldly, some timorously, but all found themselves at last on the level ground.

As the brothers travelled on they heard a wren chirping, and they saw that one of their number had a blue hole in his heart. Farther on they found a hawk's feather, which they tied in the hair of the youngest. They came at length to a deserted village on the shores of an inlet, and took possession of one of the huts. For food they ate some mussels, and having satisfied their hunger they set out to explore the settlement. Nothing rewarded their search but an old canoe, moss-grown and covered with nettles. When they had removed the weeds and scraped off the moss they repaired it, and the mischievous one who had led them into the fire made a bark bailer for it, on which he carved the representation of a bird. Another, who had in his hair a bunch of feathers, took a pole and jumped into the canoe. The rest followed, and the canoe slid away from the shore. Soon they came in sight of a village where a *shaman* was performing.

Attracted by the noise and the glow of the fire, the warrior at the bow stepped ashore and advanced to see what was going on. "Now," he heard the *shaman* say, "the chief Supernatural-being-who-keeps-the-bow-off is coming ashore." The Indian was ashamed to hear himself thus mistakenly, as he thought, referred to as a supernatural being, and returned to the canoe. The next one advanced to the village. "Chief Hawk-hole is coming ashore," said the *shaman*. The Indian saw the blue hole at his heart, and he also was ashamed, and returned to his brothers. The third was named Supernatural-being-on-whom-the-daylight-rests, the fourth Supernatural-being-on-the-water-on-whom-is-sunshine, the fifth Supernatural-puffin-on-the-water, the sixth Hawk-with-one-feather-sticking-out-of the water, the seventh Wearing-clouds-around-his-neck, the eighth Supernatural-being-with-the-big-eyes, the ninth Supernatural-being-lying-on-his-back-in-the-canoe, and the eldest, and last, Supernatural-being-half-of-whose-words-are-raven. Each as he heard his name pronounced returned to the canoe. When they had all heard the *shaman,* and were assembled once more, the eldest brother said, "We have indeed become supernatural people," which was quite true, for by burning themselves in the fire they had reached the Land of Souls.[1]

THE SUPERNATURAL SISTER

The ten brothers floated round the coast till they reached another village. Here they took on board a woman whose arms had been accidentally burned by her husband, who mistook them for the arms of someone embracing his wife. The woman was severely burned and was in great distress. The supernatural brothers made a crack in the bottom of the canoe and told the woman to place her hands in it. Her wounds were immediately healed. They called her their sister, and seated her in the canoe to bail out the water. When they came to the Djū, the stream near which dwelt Fine-weather-woman,[2] the latter came and talked to them, repeating the names which the *shaman* had given them, and calling their sister Supernatural-woman-who-does-the-bailing.

"Paddle to the island you see in the distance," she added. "The wizard who lives there is he who paints those who are to become supernatural beings. Go to him and he will paint you. Dance four nights in your canoe and you will be finished."

---

[1] This myth would appear to explain the fancied resemblance between smoke and the shadowy or vaporous substance of which spirits or ghosts are supposed to be composed.

[2] See page 114.

They did as she bade them, and the wizard dressed them in a manner becoming to their position as supernatural beings. He gave them dancing hats, dancing skirts, and puffin-beak rattles, and drew a cloud over the outside of their canoe.

THE BIRTH OF SÎÑ

The Haida of British Columbia and the Queen Charlotte Islands possess a striking myth relating to the incarnation of the Sky-god, their principal deity. The daughter of a certain chief went one day to dig in the beach. After she had worked some time she dug up a cockleshell. She was about to throw it to one side when she thought she heard a sound coming from it like that of a child crying. Examining the shell, she found a small baby inside. She carried it home and wrapped it in a warm covering, and tended it so carefully that it grew rapidly and soon began to walk.

She was sitting beside the child one day when he made a movement with his hand as if imitating the drawing of a bowstring, so to please him she took a copper bracelet from her arm and hammered it into the shape of a bow, which she strung and gave him along with two arrows. He was delighted with the tiny weapon, and immediately set out to hunt small game with it. Every day he returned to his foster mother with some trophy of his skill. One day it was a goose, another a woodpecker, and another a blue jay.

One morning he awoke to find himself and his mother in a fine new house, with gorgeous doorposts splendidly carved and illuminated in rich reds, blues, and greens. The carpenter who had raised this fine building married his mother, and was very kind to him. He took the boy down to the seashore, and caused him to sit with his face looking toward the expanse of the Pacific. And so long as the lad looked across the boundless blue there was fair weather.

His father used to go fishing, and one day Sîñ—for such was the boy's name—expressed a wish to accompany him. They obtained devil-fish for bait, and proceeded to the fishing-ground, where the lad instructed his father to pronounce certain magical formulæ, the result of which was that their fishing-line was violently agitated and their canoe pulled around an adjacent island three times. When the disturbance stopped at last they pulled in the line and dragged out a monster covered with piles of halibut.

One day Sîñ went out wearing a wren-skin. His mother beheld him rise in stature until he soared above her and brooded like a bank of shining clouds over the ocean. Then he descended and donned the skin of a blue jay. Again he rose over the sea, and shone resplendently. Once more he soared upward, wearing the skin of a woodpecker, and the waves reflected a colour as of fire.

Then he said: "Mother, I shall see you no more. I am going away from you. When the sky looks like my face painted by my father there will be no wind. Then the fishing will be good."

His mother bade him farewell, sadly, yet with the proud knowledge that she had nurtured a divinity. But her sorrow increased when her husband intimated that it was time for him to depart as well. Her supernatural son and husband, however, left her a portion of their power. For when she sits by the inlet and loosens her robe the wind scurries down between the banks and the waves are ruffled with tempest; and the more she loosens the garment the greater is the storm. They call her in the Indian tongue Fine-weather-woman. But she dwells mostly in the winds, and when the cold morning airs draw up from the sea landward she makes an offering of feathers to her glorious son. The feathers are flakes of snow, and they serve to remind him that the world is weary for a glimpse of his golden face.

MASTER-CARPENTER AND SOUTHEAST

A Haida myth relates how Master-carpenter, a supernatural being, went to war with South-east (the southeast wind) at Sqa-i, the town lying farthest south on the Queen Charlotte Islands. The southeast wind is particularly rude and boisterous on that coast, and it was with the intention of punishing him for his violence that Master-carpenter challenged him. First of all, however, he set about building a canoe for himself. The first one he made split, and he was obliged to throw it away. The second also split, notwithstanding the fact that he had made it stouter than the other. Another and another he built, making each one stronger than the last, but every attempt ended in failure, and at last, exceedingly vexed at his unskillfulness, he was on the point of giving up the task. He would have done so, indeed, but for the intervention of Greatest Fool. Hitherto Master-carpenter had been trying to form two canoes from one log by means of wedges. Greatest Fool stood watching him for a time, amused at his clumsiness, and finally showed him that he ought to use bent wedges. And though he was perhaps the last person from whom Master-carpenter might expect to learn anything, the unsuccessful builder of canoes adopted the suggestion, with the happiest results. When at length he was satisfied that he had made a good canoe he let it down into the water, and sailed off in search of South-east.

By and by he floated right down to his enemy's abode, and when he judged himself to be above it he rose in the canoe and flung out a challenge. There was no reply. Again he called, and this time a rapid current began to float past him, bearing on its surface a quantity of seaweed. The shrewd Master-carpenter fancied he saw the matted hair of his enemy floating among the seaweed. He seized hold of it, and after it came South-east. The latter in a great passion began to call on his nephews to help him. The first to be summoned was Red-storm-cloud. Immediately a deep red suffused the sky. Then the stormy tints died away, and the wind rose with a harsh murmur. When this wind had reached its full strength another was summoned, Taker-off-of-the-treetops. The blast increased to a hurricane, and the treetops were blown off and carried away and fell thickly about the canoe, where Master-carpenter was making use of his magic arts to protect himself. Again another wind was called up, Pebble-rattler, who set the stones and sand flying about as he shrieked in answer to the summons. Maker-of-the-thick-sea-mist came next, the spirit of the fog which strikes terror into the hearts of those at sea, and he was followed by a numerous band of other nephews, each to be dreaded more than the last. Finally Tidal-wave came and covered Master-carpenter with water, so that he was obliged to give in. Relinquishing his hold on South-east, he managed to struggle to the shore. It was said by some that South-east died, but the *shamans*, who ought to know, say that he returned to his own place.

South-east's mother was named Tomorrow, and the Indians say that if they utter that word they will have bad weather, for South-east does not like to hear his mother's name used by anyone else.

THE BEAVER AND THE PORCUPINE

This is the tale of a feud between the beavers and the porcupines. Beaver had laid in a plentiful store of food, but Porcupine had failed to do so, and one day when the former was out hunting the latter went to his lodge and stole his provisions. When Beaver returned he found that his food was gone, and he questioned Porcupine about the matter.

"Did you steal my food?" he asked.

"No," answered Porcupine. "One cannot steal food from supernatural beings, and you and I both possess supernatural powers."

Of course this was mere bluff on the part of Porcupine, and it in nowise deceived his companion.

"You stole my food!" said Beaver angrily, and he tried to seize Porcupine with his teeth. But the sharp spines of the latter disconcerted him, though he was not easily repulsed. For a time he fought furiously, but at length he was forced to retreat, with his face covered with quills from his spiny adversary. His friends and relatives greeted him sympathetically. His father summoned all the Beaver People, told them of the injuries his son had received, and bade them avenge the honour of their clan. The people at once repaired to the abode of Porcupine, who, from the fancied security of his lodge, heaped insults and abuse on them. The indignant Beaver People pulled his house down about his ears, seized him, and carried him, in spite of his threats and protests, to a desolate island, where they left him to starve.

It seemed to Porcupine that he had not long to live. Nothing grew on the island save two trees, neither of which was edible, and there was no other food within reach. He called loudly to his friends to come to his assistance, but there was no answer. In vain he summoned all the animals who were related to him. His cries never reached them.

When he had quite given up hope he fancied he heard something whisper to him: "Call upon Cold-weather, call upon North-wind." At first he did not understand, but thought his imagination must be playing tricks with him. Again the voice whispered to him: "Sing North songs, and you will be saved." Wondering much, but with hope rising in his breast, Porcupine did as he was bidden, and raised his voice in the North songs. "Let the cold weather come," he sang, "let the water be smooth."

THE FINDING OF PORCUPINE

After a time the weather became very cold, a strong wind blew from the north, and the water became smooth with a layer of ice. When it was sufficiently frozen to bear the weight of the Porcupine People they crossed over to the island in search of their brother. They were greatly rejoiced to see him, but found him so weak that he could hardly walk, and he had to be carried to his father's lodge.

When they wanted to know why Beaver had treated him so cruelly he replied that it was because he had eaten Beaver's food. The Porcupine People, thinking this a small excuse, were greatly incensed against the beavers, and immediately declared war on them. But the latter were generally victorious, and the war by and by came to an inglorious end for the porcupines. The spiny tribe still, however, imagined that they had a grievance against Beaver, and plotted to take his life. They carried him to the top of a tall tree, thinking that as the beavers could not climb he would be in the same plight as their brother had been on the island. But by the simple expedient of eating the tree downward from the top Beaver was enabled to return to his home.

THE DEVIL-FISH'S DAUGHTER

A Haida Indian was sailing in his canoe with his two children and his wife at low tide. They had been paddling for some time, when they came to a place where some devil-fish stones lay, and they could discern the devil-fish's tracks and see where its food was lying piled up. The man, who was a *shaman,* landed upon the rocks with the intention of finding and killing the devil-fish, but while he was searching for it the monster suddenly emerged from its hole and dragged him through the aperture into its den. His wife and children, believing him to be dead, paddled away.

The monster which had seized the man was a female devil-fish, and she dragged him far below into the precincts of the town where dwelt her father, the devil-fish chief, and there he married the devil-fish which had captured him. Many years passed, and at length the man became homesick and greatly desired to see his wife and family once more. He begged the chief to let him go, and after some demur his request was granted.

The *shaman* departed in one canoe, and his wife, the devil-fish's daughter, in another. The canoes were magical, and sped along of themselves. Soon they reached his father's town by the aid of the enchanted craft. He had brought much wealth with him from the devil-fish kingdom, and with this he traded and became a great chief. Then his children found him and came to him. They were grown up, and to celebrate his home-coming he held a great feast. Five great feasts he held, one after another, and at each of them his children and his human wife were present.

But the devil-fish wife began to pine for the sea-life. One day while her husband and she sat in his father's house he began to melt. At the same time the devil-fish wife disappeared betwixt the planks of the floor-ing. her husband then assumed the devil-fish form, and a second soft, slimy body followed the first through the planks. The devil-fish wife and her husband had returned to her father's realm.

This myth, of course, approximates to those of the seal-wives who escape from their mortal husbands, and the swan- and other bird-brides who, pining for their natural environment, take wing one fine day and leave their earth-mates.

CHINOOK TALES

The Chinooks formerly dwelt on Columbia River, from the Dalles to its mouth, and on the Lower Williamette. With the exception of a few indi-viduals, they are now extinct, but their myths have been successfully collected and preserved. They were the natives of the northwest coast, cunning in bargaining, yet dwelling on a communal plan. Their chief physical characteristic was a high and narrow forehead artificially flat-tened. Concerning this people Professor Daniel Wilson says:

"The Chinooks are among the most remarkable of the flat-headed Indians, and carry the process of cranial distortion to the greatest excess. They are in some respects a superior race, making slaves of other tribes, and evincing considerable skill in such arts as are required in their wild forest and coast life. Their chief war-implements are bows and arrows, the former made from the yew-tree, and the latter feathered and pointed with bone. Their canoes are hollowed out of the trunk of the cedar-tree,

which attains to a great size in that region, and are frequently orna-
mented with much taste and skill. In such a canoe the dead Chinook
chief is deposited, surrounded with all the requisites for war, or the
favourite occupations of life: presenting a correspondence in his sepul-
chral rites to the ancient pagan viking, who, as appears alike from the
contents of the Scandinavian *Skibssaetninger* and from the narratives of
the sagas, was interred or consumed in his war-galley, and the form of
that favourite scene of ocean triumphs perpetuated in the earth-work
that covered his ashes."

THE STORY OF BLUE JAY AND IOI

The Chinooks tell many stories of Blue Jay, the tricky, mischievous
totem-bird, and among these tales there are three which are concerned
with his sister Ioi. Blue Jay, whose disposition resembled that of the bird
he symbolized, delighted in tormenting Ioi by deliberately misinterpret-
ing her commands, and by repeating at every opportunity his favourite
phrase, "Ioi is always telling lies."

In the first of the trilogy Ioi requested her brother to take a wife from
among the dead, to help her with her work in house and field. To this
Blue Jay readily assented, and he took for his spouse a chieftain's daughter who had been recently buried. But Ioi's request that his wife should
be an old one he disregarded.

"Take her to the Land of the Supernatural People," said Ioi, when she
had seen her brother's bride, "and they will restore her to life."

Blue Jay set out on his errand, and after a day's journey arrived with
his wife at a town inhabited by the Supernatural Folk.

"How long has she been dead?" they asked him, when he stated his
purpose in visiting them.

"A day," he replied.

The Supernatural People shook their heads.

"We cannot help you," said they. "You must travel to the town where
people are restored who have been dead for a day."

Blue Jay obediently resumed his journey, and at the end of another day
he reached the town to which he had been directed, and told its inhabitants why he had come.

"How long has she been dead?" they asked.

"Two days," said he.

"Then we can do nothing," replied the Supernatural Folk, "for we can
only restore people who have been dead one day. However, you can go
to the town where those are brought to life who have been dead two
days."

Another day's journey brought Blue Jay and his wife to the third town.
Again he found himself a day late, and was directed to a fourth town,

and from that one to yet another. At the fifth town, however, the Supernatural People took pity on him, and recovered his wife from death. Blue Jay they made a chieftain among them, and conferred many honours upon him.

After a time he got tired of living in state among the Supernatural People, and returned home.

When he was once more among his kindred his young brother-in-law, the chief's son, learnt that his sister was alive and married to Blue Jay.

Hastily the boy carried the news to his father, the old chief, who sent a message to Blue Jay demanding his hair in payment for his wife. The messenger received no reply, and the angry chief gathered his people round him and led them to Blue Jay's lodge. On their approach Blue Jay turned himself into a bird and flew away, while his wife swooned. All the efforts of her kindred could not bring the woman round, and they called on her husband to return. It was in vain, however: Blue Jay would not come back, and his wife journeyed finally to the Land of Souls.

THE MARRIAGE OF IOI

The second portion of the trilogy relates how the Ghost-people, setting out one night from the Shadow-land to buy a wife, took Ioi, the sister of Blue Jay, who disappeared before morning. After a year had elapsed her brother decided to go in search of her. But though he inquired the way to the Ghost-country from all manner of birds and beasts, he got a satisfactory answer from none of them, and would never have arrived at his destination at all had he not been carried thither at last by supernatural means.

In the Ghost-country he found his sister, surrounded by heaps of bones, which she introduced to him as his relatives by marriage. At certain times these relics would attain a semblance of humanity, but instantly became bones again at the sound of a loud voice.

A FISHING EXPEDITION IN SHADOW-LAND

At his sister's request Blue Jay went fishing with his young brother-in-law. Finding that when he spoke in a loud tone he caused the boy to become a heap of bones in the canoe, Blue Jay took a malicious pleasure in reducing him to that condition. It was just the sort of trick he loved to play.

The fish they caught were nothing more than leaves and branches, and Blue Jay, in disgust, threw them back into the water. But, to his chagrin, when he returned his sister told him that they were really fish, and that he ought not to have flung them away. However, he consoled himself with the reflection, "Ioi is always telling lies."

Besides teasing Ioi, he played many pranks on the inoffensive Ghosts.

Sometimes he would put the skull of a child on the shoulders of a man, and *vice versa,* and take a mischievous delight in the ludicrous result when they came "alive."

On one occasion, when the prairies were on fire, Ioi bade her brother extinguish the flames. For this purpose she gave him five buckets of water, warning him that he must not pour it on the burning prairies until he came to the fourth of them. Blue Jay disobeyed her, as he was wont to do, and with dire results, for when he reached the fifth prairie he found he had no water to pour on it. While endeavouring to beat out the flames he was so seriously burned that he died, and returned to the Ghosts as one of themselves, but without losing his mischievous propensities.

BLUE JAY AND IOI GO VISITING

The third tale of the trilogy tells how Blue Jay and Ioi went to visit their friends. The Magpie was the first to receive the visitors, and by means of magic he provided food for them. Putting a salmon egg into a kettle of boiling water, he placed the kettle on the fire, and immediately it was full of salmon eggs, so that when they had eaten enough Blue Jay and Ioi were able to carry a number away.

On the following day the Magpie called for the kettle they had borrowed. Blue Jay tried to entertain his visitor in the same magical fashion as the latter had entertained him. But his attempt was so ludicrous that the Magpie could not help laughing at him.

The pair's next visit was to the Duck, who obtained food for them by making her children dive for trout. Again there was twice as much as they could eat, and Blue Jay and Ioi carried away the remainder on a mat. During the return visit of the Duck Blue Jay tried to emulate this feat also, using Ioi's children instead of the ducklings. His attempt was again unsuccessful.

The two visited in turn the Black Bear, the Beaver, and the Seal, all of whom similarly supplied refreshment for them in a magical manner. But Blue Jay's attempts at imitating these creatures were futile.

A visit to the Shadows concluded the round, and the adventurers returned home.

THE HEAVEN-SOUGHT BRIDE

A brother and sister left destitute by the death of their father, a chief of the Chinooks, were forced to go hunting sea-otters every day to obtain a livelihood. As they hunted the mists came down, and with them the Supernatural People, one of whom became enamoured of the girl. The ghostly husband sent his wife gifts of stranded timber and whale-meat, so that when her son was born she might want for nothing. The mischievous Blue Jay, hearing of the abundance of meat in the young chief's house, apprised his own chief of the circumstance and brought all the village to share it. The Supernatural People, annoyed that their bounty should be thus misused, abducted the young chief's sister, along with her child.

The woman's aunt, the Crow, gathered many potentilla and other roots, placed them in her canoe, and put out to sea. She came to the country of the Supernatural Folk, and when they saw her approaching they all ran down to the beach to greet her. They greedily snatched at the roots she had brought with her and devoured them, eating the most succulent and throwing away those that were not so much to their taste. The Crow soon found her niece, who laughed at her for bringing such fare to such a land.

"Do you think they are men that you bring them potentilla roots?" she cried. "They only eat certain of the roots you have fetched hither because they have magical properties. The next time you come bring the sorts of roots they seized upon—and you can also bring a basket of potentilla roots for me."

THE WHALE-CATCHER

She then called upon a dog which was gambolling close at hand.

"Take this dog," she said to the Crow. "It belongs to your grand-nephew. When you come near the shore say, 'Catch a whale, dog,' and see what happens."

The Crow bade farewell to her niece, and reentering her canoe, steered for the world of mortals again. The dog lay quietly in the stern. When about halfway across the Crow recollected her niece's advice.

"Catch a whale, good dog," she cried encouragingly.

The dog arose, and at that moment a whale crossed the path of the canoe. The dog sank his teeth in the great fish, and the frail bark rocked violently.

"Hold him fast, good fellow!" cried the Crow excitedly. "Hold him fast!" But the canoe tossed so dangerously and shipped so much water that in great fright she bade the dog let go. He did so, and lay down in the stern again.

The Crow arrived at the world of men once more, and after landing turned round to call her wonderful dog ashore. But no trace of him was visible. He had disappeared.

Once more the Crow gathered many roots and plants, taking special care to collect a good supply of the sort of the Supernatural People were fond of, and gathering only a small basket of potentilla. For the second time she crossed over to the land of the Divine Beings, who, on espying her succulent cargo, devoured it at once. She carried the potentilla roots to her niece, and when in her house noticed the dog she had received and lost. Her niece informed her that she should not have ordered the animal to seize the whale in mid-ocean, but should have waited until she was nearer the land. The Crow departed once more, taking the dog with her.

When they approached the land of men the Crow called to the animal to catch a whale, but it stirred not. Then the Crow poured some water over him, and he started up and killed a large whale, the carcass of which drifted onto the beach, when the people came down and cut it up for food.

THE CHINOOKS VISIT THE SUPERNATURALS

Some time after this the young chief expressed a desire to go to see his sister, so his people manned a large canoe and set forth. The chief of the Supernatural People, observing their approach, warned his subjects that the mortals might do something to their disadvantage, and by means of magic he covered the sea with ice. The air became exceedingly cold, so cold, indeed, that Blue Jay, who had accompanied the young chief, leapt into the water. At this one of the Supernatural People on shore laughed and cried out: "Ha, ha! Blue Jay has drowned himself!" At this taunt the young chief in the canoe arose, and, taking the ice which covered the surface of the sea, cast it away. At sight of such power the Supernatural Folk became much alarmed.

The chief and his followers now came to land, and, walking up the beach, found it deserted. Not a single Supernatural Person was to be seen. Espying the chief's house, however, the Chinooks approached it. It was guarded by sea-lions, one at each side of the door. The chief cautiously warned his people against attempting an entrance. But the irrepressible Blue Jay tried to leap past the sea-lions, and got severely bitten for his pains. Howling dismally, he rushed seaward. The young chief, annoyed that the Divine Beings should have cause for laughter against any of his people, now darted forward, seized the monsters one in each hand, and hurled them far away.

At this second feat the Supernatural Folk set up a hubbub of rage and dismay, which was turned to loud laughter when Blue Jay claimed the deed as his, loudly chanting his own praises. The Chinooks, taking heart, entered the lodge. But the Supernatural Folk vanished, leaving only the chief's sister behind.

The Chinooks had had nothing to eat since leaving their own country, and Blue Jay, who, like most worthless folk, was always hungry, complained loudly that he was famished. His brother Robin sullenly ordered him to be silent. Suddenly a Supernatural Being with a long beak emerged from under the bed, and, splitting wood with his beak, kindled a large fire.

"Robin," said Blue Jay, "that is the spirit of our great-grandfather's slave."

Soon the house was full of smoke, and a voice was heard calling out for the Smoke-eater. An individual with an enormous belly made his appearance, and swallowed all the smoke, so that the house became light. A small dish was brought, containing only one piece of meat. But the mysterious voice called for the Whale-meat-cutter, who appeared, and sliced the fragment so with his beak that the plate was full to overflowing. Then he blew upon it, and it became a large canoe full of meat, which the Chinooks finished, much to the amazement of the Supernatural People.

THE FOUR TESTS

After a while a messenger from the Divine People approached and asked to be told whether the Indians would accept a challenge to a diving contest, the defeated to lose their lives. This was agreed to, and Blue Jay was selected to dive for the Chinooks. He had taken the precaution of placing some bushes in his canoe, which he threw into the water before diving with his opponent, a woman. When his breath gave out he came to the surface, concealing his head under the floating bushes. Then he sank into the water again, and cried to his opponent: "Where are you?" "Here I am," she replied. Four times did Blue Jay cunningly come up for breath, hidden beneath the bushes, and on diving for the last time he found the woman against whom he was pitted lying at the bottom of the sea, almost unconscious. He took his club, which he had concealed beneath his blanket, and struck her on the nape of the neck. Then he rose and claimed the victory.

The Supernatural People, much chagrined, suggested a climbing contest, to which Blue Jay readily agreed, but he was warned that if he was beaten he would be dashed to pieces. He placed upright a piece of ice which was so high that it reached the clouds. The Supernaturals matched a chipmunk against him. When the competitors had reached a certain height Blue Jay grew tired, so he used his wings and flew upward. The chipmunk kept her eyes closed and did not notice the deception. Blue Jay hit her on the neck with his club, so that she fell, and Blue Jay was adjudged the winner.

A shooting match was next proposed by the exasperated Supernaturals, in which the persons engaged were to shoot at one another. This the Chinooks won by taking a beaver as their champion and tying a millstone in front of him. A sweating match was also won by the Chinooks taking ice with them into the superheated caves where the contest took place.

As a last effort to shame the Chinooks the Divine People suggested that the two chiefs should engage in a whale-catching contest. This was agreed to, and the Supernatural chief's wife, after warning them, placed Blue Jay and Robin under her armpits to keep them quiet. As they descended to the beach, she said to her brother: "Four whales will pass you, but do not harpoon any until the fifth appears."

Robin did as he was bid, but the woman had a hard time in keeping the curious Blue Jay hidden. The four whales passed, but the young chief took no heed. Then the fifth slid by. He thrust his harpoon deep into its blubber, and cast it ashore. The Supernatural chief was unsuccessful in his attempts, and so the Chinooks won again. On the result being known Blue Jay could no longer be restrained, and, falling from under the woman's arm, he was drowned.

On setting out for home the chief was advised to tie Robin's blanket to a magical rope with which his sister provided him. When the Chinooks were in the middle of the ocean the Supernatural People raised a great storm to encompass their destruction. But the charm the chief's sister had given them proved efficacious, and they reached their own land in safety.

Blue Jay's death may be regarded as merely figurative, for he appears in many subsequent Chinook tales.

This myth is undoubtedly one of the class which relates to the "Harrying of Hades." See the remarks at the conclusion of the myth of "The Thunderer's Son-in-Law."

THE THUNDERER'S SON-IN-LAW

There were five brothers who lived together. Four of them were accustomed to spend their days in hunting elk, while the fifth, who was the youngest, was always compelled to remain at the camp. They lived amicably enough, save that the youngest grumbled at never being able to go to the hunting. One day as the youth sat brooding over his grievance the silence was suddenly broken by a hideous din which appeared to come from the region of the doorway. He was at a loss to understand the cause of it, and anxiously wished for the return of his brothers. Suddenly there appeared before him a man of gigantic size, strangely apparelled. He demanded food, and the frightened boy, remembering that they were well provided, hastily arose to satisfy the stranger's desires. He brought out an ample supply of meat and tallow, but was astonished to find that the strange being lustily called for more. The youth, thoroughly terrified, hastened to gratify the monster's craving, and the giant ate steadily on, hour after hour, until the brothers returned at the end of the day to discover the glutton devouring the fruits of their hunting. The monster appeared not to heed the brothers, but, anxious to satisfy his enormous appetite, he still ate. A fresh supply of meat had been secured, and this the brothers placed before him. He continued to gorge himself throughout the night and well into the next day. At last the meat was at an end, and the brothers became alarmed. What next would the insatiable creature demand? They approached him and told him that only skins remained, but he replied: "What shall I eat, grandchildren, now that there are only skins and you?" They did not appear to understand him until they had questioned him several times. On realizing that the glutton meant to devour them, they determined to escape, so, boiling the skins, which they set before him, they fled through a hole in the hut. Outside they placed a dog, and told him to send the giant in the direction opposite to that which they had taken. Night fell, and the monster slept, while the dog kept a weary vigil over the exit by which his masters had escaped. Day dawned as the giant crept through the gap. He asked the dog: "Which way went your masters?" The animal replied by setting his head in the direction opposite to the true one. The giant observed the sign, and went on the road the dog indicated. After proceeding for some distance he found that the young men could not have gone that way, so he returned to the hut, to find the dog still there. Again he questioned the animal, who merely repeated his previous movement. The monster once more set out, but, unable to discover the fugitives, he again returned. Three times he repeated these fruitless journeys. At last he succeeded in getting on to the right path, and shortly came within sight of the brothers.

THE THUNDERER

Immediately they saw their pursuer they endeavoured to outrun him, but without avail. The giant gained ground, and soon overtook the eldest, whom he slew. He then made for the others, and slew three more. The youngest only was left. The lad hurried on until he came to a river, on the bank of which was a man fishing, whose name was the Thunderer. This person he implored to convey him to the opposite side. After much hesitation the Thunderer agreed, and, rowing him over the stream, he commanded the fugitive to go to his hut, and returned to his nets. By this time the monster had gained the river, and on seeing the fisherman he asked to be ferried over also. The Thunderer at first refused, but was eventually persuaded by the offer of a piece of twine. Afraid that the boat might capsize, the Thunderer stretched himself across the river, and commanded the giant to walk over his body. The monster, unaware of treachery, readily responded, but no sooner had he reached the Thunderer's legs than the latter set them apart, thus precipitating him into the water. His hat also fell in after him. The Thunderer now gained his feet, and watched the giant drifting helplessly down the stream. He did not wish to save the monster, for he believed him to be an evil spirit. "Okulam [Noise of Surge] will be your name," he said. "Only when the storm is raging will you be heard. When the weather is very bad your hat will also be heard." As he concluded this prophecy the giant disappeared from sight. The Thunderer then gathered his nets together and went to his hut. The youth whom he had saved married his daughter, and continued to remain with him. One day the youth desired to watch his father-in-law fishing for whales. His wife warned him against doing so. He paid no heed to her warning, however, but went to the sea, where he saw the Thunderer struggling with a whale. His father-in-law flew into a great rage, and a furious storm arose. The Thunderer looked toward the land, and immediately the storm increased in fury, with thunder and lightning, so he threw down his dip-net and departed for home, followed by his son-in-law.

STORM-RAISING

On reaching the house the young man gathered some pieces of coal and climbed a mountain. There he blackened his face, and a high wind arose which carried everything before it. His father-in-law's house was blown away, and the Thunderer, seeing that it was hopeless to attempt to save anything from the wreck, commanded his daughter to seek for her husband. She hurried up the mountainside, where she found him, and told him he was the cause of all the destructions, but concluded: "Father says you may look at him tomorrow when he catches whales." He followed his wife back to the valley and washed his face. Immediately he had done so the storm abated. Going up to his father-in-law, he said: "Tomorrow I shall go down to the beach, and you shall see me catching whales." Then the Thunderer and he rebuilt their hut. On the following morning they went down to the seashore together. The young man cast his net into the sea. After a little while a whale entered the net. The youth quickly pulled the net toward him, reached for the whale, and flung it at the feet of his father-in-law. Thunderer was amazed, and called to him: "Ho, ho, my son-in-law, you are just as I was when I was a young man."

THE BEAST COMRADES

Soon after this the Thunderer's daughter gave birth to two sons. The Thunderer sent the young man into the woods to capture two wolves with which he used to play when a boy. The son-in-law soon returned with the animals, and threw them at the feet of the Thunderer. But they severely mauled the old man, who, seeing that they had forgotten him, cried piteously to his son-in-law to carry them back to the forest. Shortly after this he again despatched his son-in-law in search of two bears with which he had also been friendly. The young man obeyed. But the bears treated the old man as the wolves had done, so he likewise returned them to their native haunts. For the third time the son-in-law went into the forest, for two grizzly bears, and when he saw them he called: "I come to carry you away." The bears instantly came toward him and suffered themselves to be carried before the Thunderer. But they also had forgotten their former playmate, and immediately set upon him, so that the young man was compelled to return with them to the forest. Thunderer had scarcely recovered from this last attack when he sent his son-in-law into the same forest after two panthers, which in his younger days had also been his companions. Without the slightest hesitation the young man arose and went into the wood, where he met the panthers. He called to them in the same gentle manner: "I come to take you away." The animals seemed to understand, and followed him. But Thunderer was dismayed when he saw how wild they had grown. They would not allow him to tame them, and after suffering their attack he sent them back to the forest. This ended the Thunderer's exciting pastime.

THE TESTS

The Thunderer then sent his son-in-law to split a log of wood. When this had been done he put the young man's strength to the test by placing him within the hollow trunk and closing the wood around him. But the young man succeeded in freeing himself, and set off for the hut carrying the log with him. On reaching his home he dropped the wood before the door, and caused the earth to quake. The Thunderer jumped up in alarm and ran to the door rejoicing in the might of his son-in-law. "Oh, my son-in-law," he cried, "you are just as I was when I was young!" The two continued to live together and the young man's sons grew into manhood. One day the Thunderer approached his son-in-law and said: "Go to the Supernatural Folk and bring me their hoops."

THE SPIRIT-LAND

The son-in-law obeyed. He travelled for a long distance, and eventually reached the land of the spirits. They stood in a circle, and he saw that they played with a large hoop. He then remembered that he must secure the hoop. But he was afraid to approach them, as the light of the place dazzled him. He waited until darkness had set in, and, leaving his hiding-place, dashed through the circle and secured the hoop. The Supernatural People pursued him with torches. Just as this was taking place his wife remembered him. She called to her children: "Now whip your grandfather." This they did, while the old man wept. This chastisement brought rain upon the Supernatural People and extinguished their torches. They dared not pursue the young man farther, so they returned to their country. The adventurer was now left in peace to continue his homeward journey. He handed over the hoop to Thunderer, who now sent him to capture the targets of the Spirit Folk. The son-in-law gladly undertook the journey, and again entered the bright region of Spirit-land. He found the Supernaturals shooting at the targets, and when night had fallen he picked them up and ran away. The spirits lit their torches and followed him. His wife once more was reminded of her absent hus-band, and commanded her sons to repeat the punishment upon their grandfather. The rain recommenced and the torches of the pursuers were destroyed. The young man returned in peace to his dwelling and placed the targets before his father-in-law. He had not been long home before a restless spirit took possession of him. He longed for further adventure, and at last decided to set out in quest of it. Arraying himself in his fine necklaces of teeth and strapping around his waist two quivers of arrows, he bade farewell to his wife and sons. He journeyed until he reached a large village, which consisted of five rows of houses. These he carefully inspected. The last house was very small, but he entered it. He was met by two old women, who were known as the Mice. Immediately they saw him they muttered to each other: "Oh, now Blue Jay will make another chief unhappy." On the young man's arrival in the village Blue Jay became conscious of a stranger in the midst of the people. He straight-away betook himself to the house of the Mice. He then returned to his chief, saying that a strange chief wished to hold a shooting match. Blue Jay's chief seemed quite willing to enter into the contest with the stranger, so he sent Blue Jay back to the house to inform the young chief of his willingness. Blue Jay led the stranger down to the beach where the targets stood. Soon the old chief arrived and the shooting match began. But the adventurer's skill could not compare with the old chief's, who finally defeated him. Blue Jay now saw his opportunity. He sprang upon the stranger, tore out his hair, cut off his head, and severed the limbs from his body. He carried the pieces to the house and hung up the head. At nightfall the Mice fed the head and managed to keep it alive. This process of feeding went on for many months, the old women never tiring of their task. A full year had passed, and the unfortunate adventurer's sons began to fear for his safety. They decided to search for him. Arming themselves, they made their way to the large village in which their father was imprisoned. They entered the house of the Mice, and there saw the two old women, who asked: "Oh, chiefs, where did you come from?"

"We search for our father," they replied. But the old women warned them of Blue Jay's treachery, and advised them to depart. The young men would not heed the advice, and succeeded in drawing from the women the story of their father's fate. When they heard that Blue Jay had used their father so badly they were very angry. Blue Jay, meanwhile, had become aware of the arrival of two strangers, and he went to the small house to smell them out. There he espied the youths, and immediately returned to inform his chief of their presence in the village. The chief then sent him back to invite the strangers to a shooting match, but they ignored the invitation. Three times Blue Jay made the journey, and at last the youths looked upon him, whereupon his hair immediately took fire. He ran back to his chief and said: "Oh, these strangers are more power-ful than we are. They looked at me and my hair caught fire." The chief was amazed, and went down to the beach to await the arrival of the strangers. When the young men saw the targets they would not shoot, and declared that they were bad. They immediately drew them out of the ground and replaced them by their own, the brilliance of which dazzled the sight of their opponent. The chief was defeated. He lost his life and the people were subdued. The youths then cast Blue Jay into the river, saying as they did so: "Green Sturgeon shall be your name." Henceforth you shall not make chiefs miserable. You shall sing 'Watsetsetsetsetse,' and it shall be a bad omen." This performance over, they restored their father from his death-slumber, and spoke kindly to the Mice, saying: "Oh, you pitiful ones, you shall eat everything that is good. You shall eat berries." Then, after establishing order in this strange land, they returned to their home, accompanied by their father.

This curious story is an example of what is known in mythology as the "Harrying of Hades." The land of the supernatural or subterranean beings always exercises a profound fascination over the minds of barbarians, and such tales are invented by their storytellers for the purpose of minimizing the terrors which await them when they themselves must enter the strange country by death. The incident of the glutton would seem to show that two tales have been amalgamated, a not uncommon circumstance in prim-itive storytelling. In these stories the evil or supernatural power is invari-ably defeated, and it is touching to observe the child-like attempts of the savage to quench the dread of death, common to all mankind, by creating amusement at the ludicrous appearance of the dreadful beings whom he fears. The sons of the Thunderer are, of course, hero-gods whose effulgence confounds the powers of darkness, and to some extent they resemble the Hun-Apu and Xbalanque of the Central American *Popol Vuh,* who travel to the dark kingdom of Xibalba to rescue their father and uncle, and succeed in overthrowing its hideous denizens.[1]

---

[1] See the author's *Myths of Mexico and Peru,* in this series [p. 220]. (Available in a Dover edition)

THE MYTH OF STIKŬA

As an example of a myth as taken from the lips of the Indian by the collector we append to this series of Chinook tales the story of Stikŭa in all its pristine ingenuousness. Such a tale well exemplifies the difference of outlook between the aboriginal and the civilized mind, and exhibits the many difficulties with which collectors of such myths have to contend.

Many people were living at Nakotat. Now their chief died. He had [left] a son who was almost grown up. It was winter and the people were hungry. They had only mussels and roots to eat. Once upon a time a hunter said: "Make yourselves ready." All the men made themselves ready, and went seaward in two canoes. Then the hunter speared a sea-lion. It jumped and drifted on the water [dead]. They hauled it ashore. Blue Jay said: "Let us boil it here." They made a fire and singed it. They cut it and boiled it. Blue Jay said: "Let us eat it here, let us eat all of it." Then the people ate. Raven tried to hide a piece of meat in his mat, and carried it to the canoe. [But] Blue Jay had already seen it; he ran [after him] took it and threw it into the fire. He burned it. Then they went home. They gathered large and small mussels. In the evening they came home. Then Blue Jay shouted: "Stikŭa, fetch your mussels." Stikŭa was the name of Blue Jay's wife. Then noise of many feet [was heard], and Stikŭa and the other women came running down to the beach. They went to fetch mussels. The women came to the beach and carried the mussels to the house. Raven took care of the chief's son. The boy said: "Tomorrow I shall accompany you." Blue Jay said to him: "What do you want to do? The waves will carry you away, you will drift away; even I almost drifted away."

The next morning they made themselves ready. They went into the canoe, and the boy came down to the beach. He wanted to accompany them, and held on to the canoe. "Go to the house, go to the house," said Blue Jay. The boy went up, but he was very sad. Then Blue Jay said: "Let us leave him." The people began to paddle. Then they arrived at the sea-lion island. The hunter went ashore and speared a sea-lion. It jumped and drifted on the water [dead]. They hauled it ashore and pulled it up from the water. Blue Jay said: "Let us eat it here; let us eat all of it, else our chief's son would always want to come here." They singed it, carved it, and boiled it there. When it was done they ate it all. Raven tried to hide a piece in his hair, but Blue Jay took it out immediately and burned it. In the evening they gathered large and small mussels, and then they went home. When they approached the beach Blue Jay shouted: "Stikŭa, fetch your mussels!" Then noise of many feet [was heard]. Stikŭa and her children and all the other women came running down to the beach and carried the mussels up to the house. Blue Jay had told all those people:

"Don't tell our chief's son, else he will want to accompany us." In the evening the boy said: "Tomorrow I shall accompany you." But Blue Jay said: "What do you want to do? The waves will carry you away." But the boy replied: "I must go."

In the morning they made themselves ready for the third time. The boy went down to the beach and took hold of the canoe. But Blue Jay pushed him aside and said: "What do you want here? Go to the house." The boy cried and went up to the house. [When he turned back] Blue Jay said: "Now paddle away. We will leave him." The people began to paddle, and soon they reached the sea-lion island. The hunter went ashore and speared one large sea-lion. It jumped and drifted on the water [dead]. They hauled it toward the shore, landed, pulled it up and singed it. They finished singeing it. Then they carved it and boiled it, and when it was done they began to eat. Blue Jay said: "Let us eat it all. Nobody must speak about it, else our chief's son will always want to accompany us." A little [meat] was still left when they had eaten enough. Raven tried to take a piece with him. He tied it to his leg and said his leg was broken. Blue Jay burned all that was left over. Then he said to Raven: "Let me see your leg." He jumped at it, untied it, and found the piece of meat at Raven's leg. He took it and burned it. In the evening they gathered large and small mussels. Then they went home. When they were near home Blue Jay shouted: "Stikŭa, fetch your mussels!" Then noise of many feet [was heard], and Stikŭa [her children and the other women] came down to the beach and carried the mussels up to the house. The [women and children] and the chief's son ate the mussels all night. Then that boy said: "Tomorrow I shall accompany you." Blue Jay said: "What do you want to do? You will drift away. If I had not taken hold of the canoe I should have drifted away twice."

On the next morning they made themselves ready for the fourth time. The boy rose and made himself ready also. The people hauled their canoes into the water and went aboard. The boy tried to board a canoe also, but Blue Jay took hold of him and threw him into the water. He stood in the water up to his waist. He held the canoe, but Blue Jay struck his hands. There he stood. He cried, and cried, and went up to the house. The people went; they paddled, and soon they reached the sea-lion island. The hunter went ashore and speared a sea-lion. It jumped and drifted on the water [dead]. Again they towed it to the island, and pulled it ashore. They singed it. When they had finished singeing it they carved it and boiled it. When it was done Blue Jay said: "Let us eat it here." They ate half of it and were satiated. They slept because they had eaten too much. Blue Jay awoke first, and burned all that was left. In the evening they gathered large and small mussels and went home. When they were near the shore he shouted: "Stikŭa, fetch your mussels!" Noise of many feet [was heard] and Stikŭa [her children and the other women] came running down to the beach and carried up the mussels. The boy said: "Tomorrow I shall accompany you." But Blue Jay said: "What do you want to do? We might capsize and you would be drowned."

Early on the following morning the people made themselves ready. The boy arose and made himself ready also. Blue Jay and the people hauled their canoes down to the water. The boy tried to board, but Blue Jay threw him into the water. He tried to hold the canoe. The water reached up to his armpits. Blue Jaw struck his hands [until he let go]. Then the boy cried and cried. Blue Jay and the other people went away.

After some time the boy went up from the beach. He took his arrows and walked round a point of land. There he met a young eagle and shot it. He skinned it and tried to put the skin on. It was too small; it reached scarcely to his knees. Then he took it off, and went on. After a while he met another eagle. He shot it and it fell down. It was a white-headed eagle. He skinned it and tried the skin on, but it was too small; it reached a little below his knees. He took it off, left it, and went on. Soon he met a bald-headed eagle. He shot it twice and it fell down. He skinned it and put the skin on. It was nearly large enough for him, and he tried to fly. He could fly downward only. He did not rise. He turned back, and now he could fly. Now he went round the point seaward from Nakotat. When he had nearly gone round he smelled smoke of burning fat. When he came round the point he saw the people of his town. He alighted on top of a tree and looked down. [He saw that] they had boiled a sea-lion and that they ate it. When they had nearly finished eating he flew up. He thought: "Oh, I wish Blue Jay would see me." Then Blue Jay looked up [and saw] the bird flying about. "Ah, a bird came to get food from us." Five times the eagle circled over the fire; then it descended. Blue Jay took a piece of blubber and said: "I will give you this to eat." The bird came down, grasped the piece of meat, and flew away. "Ha!" said Blue Jay, "that bird has feet like a man." When the people had eaten enough they slept. Raven again hid a piece of meat. Toward evening they awoke and ate again; then Blue Jay burned the rest of their food. In the evening they gathered large and small mussels and went home. When the boy came home he lay down at once. They approached the village, and Blue Jay shouted: "Fetch your mussels, Stikŭa!" Noise of many feet [was heard] and Stikŭa [and the other women] ran down to the beach and carried up the mussels. They tried to rouse the boy, but he did not arise.

The next morning the people made themselves ready and launched their canoe. The chief's son stayed in bed and did not attempt to accompany them. After sunrise he rose and called the women and children and said: "Wash yourselves; be quick." The women obeyed and washed themselves. He continued: "Comb your hair." Then he put down a plank, took a piece of meat out [from under his blanket, showed it to the women, and said]: "Every day your husbands eat this." He put two pieces side by side on the plank, cut them to pieces, and greased the heads of all the women and children. Then he pulled the planks forming the walls of the houses out of the ground. He sharpened them [at one end, and] those which were very wide he split in two. He sharpened all of them. The last house of the village was that of the Raven. He did not pull out its wall-planks. He put the planks on to the backs of the women and children and said: "Go down to the beach. When you go seaward swim five times round that rock. Then go seaward. When you see sea-lions you shall kill them. But you shall not give anything to stingy people. I shall take these children down. They shall live on the sea and be my relatives."

Then he split sinews. The women went into the water and began to jump [out of the water]. They swam five times back and forth in front of the village. Then they went seaward to the place where Blue Jay and the men were boiling. Blue Jay said to the men: "What is that?" The men looked and saw the girls jumping. Five times they swam round Blue Jay's rock. Then they went seaward. After a while birds came flying to the island. Their bills were [as red] as blood. They followed [the fish]. "Ah!" said Blue Jay, "do you notice them? Whence come these numerous birds?" The Raven said: "Ha, squint-eye, they are your children; do you not recognize them?" Five times they went round the rock. Now [the boy] threw the sinews down upon the stones and said: "When Blue Jay comes to gather mussels they shall be fast [to the rocks]." And he said to the women, turning toward the sea: 'Whale-Killer will be your name. When you catch a whale you will eat it, but when you catch a sea-lion you will throw it away; but you shall not give anything to stingy people."

Blue Jay and the people were eating. Then that hunter said: "Let us go home. I am afraid we have seen evil spirits; we have never seen anything like that on this rock." Now they gathered mussels and carried along the meat which they had left over. In the evening they came near their home. [Blue Jay shouted:] "Stikŭa, fetch your mussels!" There was no sound of people. Five times he called. Now the people went ashore and [they saw that] the walls of the houses had disappeared. The people cried. Blue Jay cried also, but somebody said to him: "Be quiet, Blue Jay; if you had not been bad our chief's son would not have done so." Now they all made one house. Only Raven had one house [by himself]. He went and searched for food on the beach. He found a sturgeon. He went again to the beach and found a porpoise. Then Blue Jay went to the beach and tried to search for food. [As soon as he went out] it began to hail; the hailstones were so large [*indicating*]. He tried to gather mussels and wanted to break them off, but they did not come off. He could not break

them off. He gave up. Raven went to search on the beach and found a
seal. The others ate roots only. Thus their chief took revenge on them.

BELIEFS OF THE CALIFORNIAN TRIBES

The tribes of California afford a strange example of racial conglomera-
tion, speaking as they do a variety of languages totally distinct from one
another, and exhibiting many differences in physical appearance and
custom. Concerning their mythological beliefs Bancroft says:

"The Californian tribes, taken as a whole, are pretty uniform in the
main features of their theogonic beliefs. They seem, without exception,
to have had a hazy conception of a lofty, almost supreme being; for the
most part referred to as a Great Man, the Old Man Above, the One
Above; attributing to him, however, as is usual in such cases, nothing but
the vaguest and most negative functions and qualities. The real practical
power that most interested them, who had most to do with them and
they with him, was a demon, or body of demons, of a tolerably pronounced character. In the face of divers assertions to the effect that no
such thing as a devil proper has ever been found in savage mythology, we
would draw attention to the following extract from the *Pomo* manuscript
of Mr. Powers—a gentleman who, both by his study and by personal
investigation, has made himself one of the best qualified authorities on
the belief of the native Californian, and whose dealings have been for the
most part with tribes that have never had any friendly intercourse with
white men. Of course the thin and meagre imagination of the American
savages was not equal to the creation of Milton's magnificent imperial
Satan, or of Goethe's Mephistopheles, with his subtle intellect, his vast
powers, his malignant mirth; but in so far as the Indian fiends or devils
have the ability, they are wholly as wicked as these. They are totally bad,
they have no good thing in them, they think only evil; but they are weak
and undignified and absurd; they are as much beneath Satan as the "Big
Indians" who invent them are inferior in imagination to John Milton.

"A definite location is generally assigned to the evil one as is favourite
residence or resort; thus the Californians in the country of Siskiyou give
over Devil's Castle, its mount and lake, to the malignant spirits, and avoid
the vicinity of these places with all possible care.

"The coast tribes of Del Norte County, California, live in constant terror of a malignant spirit that takes the form of certain animals, the form
of a bat, of a hawk, of a tarantula, and so on, but especially delights in and
affects that of a screech-owl. The belief of the Russian river tribes and
others is practically identical with this.

"The Cahrocs have some conception of a great deity called Chareya,
the Old Man Above; he is wont to appear upon earth at times to some
of the most favoured sorcerers; he is described as wearing a close tunic,

with a medicine-bag, and as having long white hair that falls venerably about his shoulders. Practically, however, the Cahrocs, like the majority of Californian tribes, venerate chiefly the Coyote. Great dread is also had of certain forest-demons of nocturnal habits; these, say the Cahrocs, take the form of bears, and shoot arrows at benighted wayfarers.

"Between the foregoing outlines of Californian belief and those connected with the remaining tribes, passing south, we can detect no salient difference till we reach the Olchones, a coast tribe between San Francisco and Monterey; the sun here begins to be connected, or identified by name, with that great spirit, or rather, that Big Man, who made the earth and who rules in the sky. So we find it again both around Monterey and around San Luis Obispo; the first fruits of the earth were offered in these neighbourhoods to the great light, and his rising was greeted with cries of joy."

Father Gerónimo Boscana gives us the following account of the faith and worship of the Acagchemem tribes, who inhabit the valley and neighbourhood of San Juan Capistrano, California. We give first the version held by the *serranos,* or highlanders, of the interior country, three or four leagues inland from San Juan Capistrano:

"Before the material world at all existed there lived two beings, brother and sister, of a nature that cannot be explained; the brother living above, and his name meaning the Heavens, the sister living below, and her name signifying Earth. From the union of these two there sprang a numerous offspring. Earth and sand were the first-fruits of this marriage; then were born rocks and stones; then trees, both great and small; then grass and herbs; then animals; lastly was born a great personage called Ouiot, who was a "grand captain." By some unknown mother many children of a medicine race were born to this Ouiot. All these things happened in the north; and afterwards when men were created they were created in the north; but as the people multiplied they moved toward the south, the earth growing larger also and extending itself in the same direction.

"In process of time, Ouiot becoming old, his children plotted to kill him, alleging that the infirmities of age made him unfit any longer to govern them or attend to their welfare. So they put a strong poison in his drink, and when he drank of it a sore sickness came upon him; he rose up and left his home in the mountains, and went down to what is now the seashore, though at that time there was no sea there. His mother, whose name is the Earth, mixed him an antidote in a large shell, and set the potion out in the sun to brew; but the fragrance of it attracted the attention of the Coyote, who came and overset the shell. So Ouiot sickened to death, and though he told his children that he would shortly return and be with them again, he has never been seen since. All the people made a great pile of wood and burnt his body there, and just as the ceremony began the Coyote leaped upon the body, saying that he would burn with it; but he only tore a piece of flesh from the stomach and ate it and escaped. After that the title of the Coyote was changed from Eyacque, which means Sub-captain, to Eno, that is to say, Thief and Cannibal.

"When now the funeral rites were over, a general council was held and arrangements made for collecting animal and vegetable food; for up to this time the children and descendants of Ouiot had nothing to eat but a kind of white clay. And while they consulted together, behold a marvellous thing appeared before them, and they spoke to it, saying: "Art thou our captain, Ouiot?" But the spectre said: "Nay, for I am greater than Ouiot; my habitation is above, and my name is Chinigchinich." Then he spoke further, having been told for what they were come together: "I create all things, and I go now to make man, another people like unto you; as for you, I give you power, each after his kind, to produce all good and pleasant things. One of you shall bring rain, and another dew, and another make the acorn grow, and others other seeds, and yet others shall cause all kinds of game to abound in the land; and your children shall have this power forever, and they shall be sorcerers to the men I go to create, and shall receive gifts of them, that the game fail not and the harvests be sure." Then Chinigchinich made man; out of the clay of the lake he formed him, male and female; and the present Californians are the descendants of the one or more pairs there and thus created.

"So ends the known tradition of the mountaineers; we must now go back and take up the story anew at its beginning, as told by the *playanos,* or people of the valley of San Juan Capistrano. These say that an invisible, all-powerful being, called Nocuma, made the world and all that it contains of things that grow and move. He made it round like a ball and held it in his hands, where it rolled about a good deal at first, till he steadied it by sticking a heavy black rock called Tosaut into it, as a kind of ballast. The sea was at this time only a little stream running round the world, and so crowded with fish that their twinkling fins had no longer room to move; so great was the press that some of the more foolish fry were for effecting a landing and founding a colony upon the dry land, and it was only with the utmost difficulty that they were persuaded by their elders that the killing air and baneful sun and the want of feet must infallibly prove the destruction before many days of all who took part in such a desperate enterprise. The proper plan was evidently to improve and enlarge their present home; and to this end, principally by the aid of one very large fish, they broke the great rock Tosaut in two, finding a bladder in the centre filled with a very bitter substance. The taste of it pleased the fish, so they emptied it into the water, and instantly the water became salt and swelled up and overflowed a great part of the old earth, and made itself the new boundaries that remain to this day.

"Then Nocuma created a man, shaping him out of the soil of the earth, calling him Ejoni. A woman also the great god made, presumably out of the same material as the man, calling her Aé. Many children were born to this first pair, and their descendants multiplied over the land. The name of one of these last was Sirout, that is to say, Handful of Tobacco, and the name of his wife was Ycaiut, which means Above; and to Sirout and Ycaiut was born a son, while they lived in a place northeast about eight leagues from San Juan Capistrano. The name of this son was Ouiot, that is to say, Dominator; he grew a fierce and redoubtable warrior; haughty, ambitious, tyrannous, he extended his lordship on every side, ruling everywhere as with a rod of iron; and the people conspired against him. It was determined that he should die by poison; a piece of the rock Tousaut was ground up in so deadly a way that its mere external application was sufficient to cause death. Ouiot, notwithstanding that he held himself constantly on the alert, having been warned of his danger by a small burrowing animal called the *cucumel,* was unable to avoid his fate; a few grains of the cankerous mixture were dropped upon his breast while he slept, and the strong mineral ate its way to the very springs of his life. All the wise men of the land were called to his assistance; but there was nothing for him save to die. His body was burned on a great pile with songs of joy and dances, and the nation rejoiced.

"While the people were gathered to this end, it was thought advisable to consult on the feasibility of procuring seed and flesh to eat instead of the clay which had up to this time been the sole food of the human family. And while they yet talked together, there appeared to them, coming they knew not whence, one called Attajen, 'which name implies man, or rational being.' And Attajen, understanding their desires, chose out certain of the elders among them, and to these gave he power; one that he might cause rain to fall, to another that he might cause game to abound, and so with the rest, to each his power and gift, and to the successors of each forever. These were the first medicine-men."

Many years having elapsed since the death of Ouiot, there appeared in the same place one called Ouiamot, reputed son of Tacu and Auzar—people unknown, but natives, it is thought by Boscana, of "some distant land." This Ouiamot is better known by his great name Chinigchinich, which means Almighty. He first manifested his powers to the people on a day when they had met in congregation for some purpose or other; he appeared dancing before them crowned with a kind of high crown made of tall feathers stuck into a circlet of some kind, girt with a kind of petticoat of feathers, and having his flesh painted black and red. Thus decorated he was called the *tobet*. Having danced some time, Chinigchinich called out the medicine-men, or *puplems,* as they were called, among whom it would appear the chiefs are always numbered, and confirmed their power; telling them that he had come from the stars to instruct them in dancing and all other things, and commanding that in all their necessities they should array themselves in the *tobet,* and so dance as he had danced, supplicating him by his great name, that thus they might be granted their petitions. He taught them how to worship him, how to build *vanquechs,* or places of worship, and how to direct their conduct in various affairs of life. Then he prepared to die, and the people asked him if they should bury him; but he warned them against attempting such a thing. "If ye buried me," he said, "ye would tread upon my grave, and for that my hand would be heavy upon you; look to it, and to all your ways, for lo, I go up where the high stars are, where mine eyes shall see all the ways of men; and whosoever will not keep my commandments nor observe the things I have taught, behold, disease shall plague all his body, and no food shall come near his lips, the bear shall rend his flesh, and the crooked tooth of the serpent shall sting him."

In Lower California the Pericues were divided into two *gentes,* each of which worshipped a divinity which was hostile to the other. The tradition explains that there was a great lord in heaven, called Niparaya, who made earth and sea, and was almighty and invisible. His wife was Anayicoyondi, a goddess who, though possessing no body, bore him in a divinely mysterious manner three children, one of whom, Quaayayp, was a real man and born on earth, on the Acaragui mountains. Very powerful this young god was, and for a long time he lived with the ancestors of the Pericues, whom it is almost to be inferred that he created; at any rate we are told that he was able to make men, drawing them up out of the earth. The men at last killed their great hero and teacher, and put a crown of thorns upon his head. Somewhere or other he remains lying dead to this day; and he remains constantly beautiful, neither does his body know corruption. Blood drips constantly from his wounds; and though he can speak no more, being dead, yet there is an owl that speaks to him.

The other god was called Wac, or Tuparan. According to the Niparaya sect, this Wac had made war on their favourite god, and had been by him defeated and cast forth from heaven into a cave under the earth, of which cave the whales of the sea were the guardians. With a perverse, though not unnatural, obstinacy, the sect that took Wac or Tuparan for their great god persisted in holding ideas peculiar to themselves with regard to the truth of the foregoing story, and their account of the great war in heaven and its results differed from the other as differ the creeds of heterodox and orthodox everywhere; they ascribe, for example, part of the creation to other gods besides Niparaya.

MYTHS OF THE ATHAPASCANS

The great Athapascan family, who inhabit a vast extent of territory stretching north from the fifty-fifth parallel nearly to the Arctic Ocean, and westward to the Pacific, with cognate ramifications to the far south, are weak in mythological conceptions. Regarding them Bancroft says:[1]

"They do not seem in any of their various tribes to have a single expressed idea with regard to a supreme power. The Loucheux branch recognize a certain personage, resident in the moon, whom they supplicate for success in starting on a hunting expedition. This being once lived among them as a poor ragged boy that an old woman had found and was bringing up; and who made himself ridiculous to his fellows by making a pair of very large snow-shoes; for the people could not see what a starveling like him should want with shoes of such unusual size. Times of great scarcity troubled the hunters, and they would often have fared badly had they not invariably on such occasions come across a new broad trail that led to a head or two of freshly killed game. They were glad enough to get the game and without scruples as to its appropriation; still they felt curious as to whence it came and how. Suspicion at last pointing to the boy and his great shoes as being in some way implicated in the affair, he was watched. It soon became evident that he was indeed the benefactor of the Loucheux, and the secret hunter whose quarry had so often replenished their empty pots; yet the people were far from being adequately grateful, and continued to treat him with little kindness or respect. On one occasion they refused him a certain piece of fat—him who had so often saved their lives by his timely bounty! That night the lad disappeared, leaving only his clothes behind, hanging on a tree. He returned to them in a month, however, appearing as a man, and dressed as a man. He told them that he had taken up his home in the moon; that he would always look down with a kindly eye to their success in hunting; but he added that as a punishment for their shameless greed and ingratitude in refusing him the piece of fat, all animals should be lean the long winter through, and fat only in summer; as has since been the case.

"According to Hearne, the Tinneh believe in a kind of spirits, or fairies, called *nantena,* which people the earth, the sea, and the air, and are instrumental for both good and evil. Some of them believe in a good spirit called Tihugun, "my old friend," supposed to reside in the sun and

---

[1] *The Native Races of the Pacific States,* vol. iii.

in the moon; they have also a bad spirit, Chutsain, apparently only a personification of death, and for this reason called bad.

"They have no regular order of *shamans*; anyone when the spirit moves him may take upon himself their duties and pretentions, though some by happy chances, or peculiar cunning, are much more highly esteemed in this regard than others, and are supported by voluntary contributions. The conjurer often shuts himself in his tent and abstains from food for days till his earthly grossness thins away, and the spirits and things unseen are constrained to appear at his behest. The young Tinneh care for none of these things; the strong limb and the keen eye, holding their own well in the jostle of life, mock at the terrors of the invisible; but as the pulses dwindle with disease or age, and the knees strike together in the shadow of impending death, the *shaman* is hired to expel the evil things of which a patient is possessed. Among the Tacullies a confession is often resorted to at this stage, on the truth and accuracy of which depend the chances of a recovery."